Learning
the New Testament

Learning
the New Testament

by Ladell J. Futch

Judson Press ® Valley Forge

LEARNING THE NEW TESTAMENT

Copyright © 1978
Judson Press, Valley Forge, PA 19481

Unless otherwise indicated, Bible quotations in this volume are in accordance with the Revised Standard Version of the Bible, copyrighted 1946, 1952, 1971, 1973 © by the Division of Christian Education of the National Council of the Churches of Christ in the United States of America, and are used by permission.

Other versions of the Bible quoted in this book are:

The New English Bible, Copyright © The Delegates of the Oxford University Press and the Syndics of the Cambridge University Press, 1961, 1970.

The Living Bible, Tyndale House Publishers, Wheaton, Illinois. Used by permission.

Library of Congress Cataloging in Publication Data
Futch, Ladell J.
    Learning the New Testament.

    1. Bible. N. T.—Introductions. I. Title.
BS2330.2.F85   225.6   78-13749
ISBN 0-8170-0800-4

The name JUDSON PRESS is registered as a trademark in the U.S. Patent Office.
Printed in the U.S.A. ⊕

To Rev. Douglas L. McGuire, who
sparked my initial interest in
learning the New Testament;
Clyde Denton, who supplied vital and stern
guidance for my efforts at learning to write;
and my wife, Patricia,
who patiently endures and
encourages me through everything.

Contents

Introduction

There are so many different and often conflicting interpretations of what the New Testament says that many of us are intimidated into doubting our ability to understand it for ourselves. For too long, too many of us have allowed other people to tell us what it says; and they have told us so many different things that some of us have decided that the New Testament doesn't really tell us anything. Indeed, in some circles it has become fashionable to regard the Bible as a kind of symbolic relic of the primitive beginnings of the religion that has evolved into our modern and allegedly enlightened culture. For people in such circles it can be a very exciting and enlightening experience simply to sit back and read the New Testament as it was meant to be read.

When we learn the New Testament, we learn what God is really like and how we humans can become what we are supposed to be. That's what the writers of the New Testament learned through their own personal experiences of Jesus, and that's what they were trying to convey to those who would read what they were writing. The purpose of this book is to enable readers of today to understand better what those writers were really trying to say. No effort is made here to "teach" the New Testament; rather, this book is designed to serve as a practical and convenient study guide and reference for those persons who wish to learn the New Testament for themselves. The general idea is to make the most pertinent benefits of the best in Bible scholarship more readily accessible to the general public.

The meaty part of this book consists of brief introductions and notes on the individual writings, or books, of the New Testament. These introductions and notes are to be studied with, not instead of, the New Testament books themselves. I have taken the liberty of introducing the books in a somewhat different order from that in which they appear in the Bible. The order suggested herein is based upon a rather tentative combination of logic, classification, chronological order within classifications, and, when those aspects still failed to place them where I wanted them, personal preference. Readers, of course, are free to inject their own personal preferences and skip around to study the books in whatever order they desire.

I have also presumed to include in Section 1, "Preparing to Study the New Testament," some preliminary comments which, it is hoped, will aid readers in negotiating some of the major hazards which prevent many people from understanding, and lead others to misunderstand, the real meaning and message of the New Testament. The comments in Section 1 should provide readers with information that will bolster their self-confidence and encourage them to trust their own ability to understand what they read in their own New Testaments.

Some readers will notice and perhaps be frustrated by the absence of footnotes and other paraphernalia of documentation for the information contained herein. These have been omitted to avoid pulling the readers' attention away from the main object of our study, which is the New Testament itself. It is very appropriate, however, to acknowledge that this writer is deeply indebted to numerous sources of information, including pastors, church school teachers, divinity school professors, writers, and many other fellow Christians. Also, in addition to several modern versions of the New Testament, a number of scholarly Bible reference works have been my constant companions during the preparation of this book. It's very doubtful that any of these reference works agree with everything I have said herein. But, then, I don't agree with everything they say either!

For the benefit of those who simply must know such things, the reference materials relied upon most heavily included: *The Interpreter's Bible*, volumes 7-12 (Abingdon Press, 1951-57); *Harper's Bible Dictionary* (Harper & Row, Publishers, 1952); *The Twentieth Century Bible Commentary*, revised edition (Harper & Row, Publishers, 1955); and *An Introduction to the New Testament* by Edward W. Bauman (The Westminster Press, 1961).

Perhaps it should also be mentioned that all Bible quotations, unless otherwise noted, are from the Revised Standard Version. It is hoped that readers will use several versions, including their own personal favorite.

Now that we have all that out of the way, let's begin preparing ourselves to study the New Testament with the prayer that God will direct and bless our efforts to learn the real message that he is trying to get through to us.

Section 1
Preparing to Study the New Testament

Do your best to present yourself to God as one approved, a workman who has no need to be ashamed, rightly handling the word of truth.

2 Timothy 2:15

Section I:
Learning to Study
the New Testament

1
Learning to
Listen to the Bible

Understanding the Bible is neither as difficult as many of us believe nor as simple as some others would have us believe. The writers of the Bible were trying their best to help readers understand the supremely important truth they had personally experienced about God and human life. Some of them were better writers than others. Some of them understood the truth they were experiencing better than others. Sometimes they expressed themselves in ways quite unfamiliar to us and our age. But all of them were trying their best to record in writing, and thus preserve and share, their understanding of the truth about the character of God and the meaning of human life which they had experienced in unique and sometimes direct ways. There is no secret or hidden key to understanding the Bible. It's simply a matter of learning to "listen" to what the writers were trying to say.

To listen to the Bible requires, first of all, that we read it as the writers meant for it to be read. With few exceptions, the Bible was meant to be read book by book. Trying to understand the Bible by reading a chapter a day is like trying to understand a newspaper editorial by reading a paragraph a day. It's even worse than

14

piecemeal newspaper reading because chapters in the Bible often change in the middle of a paragraph, sometimes even in the middle of a sentence. The numbering of chapters and verses was something inflicted upon the Bible long after it was written in order to make it easier to locate specific passages. To listen to what the writers were saying, we must ignore the chapters and verses and read entire books as a whole. (In the outlines which accompany the comments on the books or combinations of books being studied as units, I have suggested places to divide the reading if more than one sitting is required to read the entire book.)

Also, in order to listen to what the Bible writers were saying, we must "hear" what they said in the context in which they said it. My wife occasionally refers to me as a silly fool. Sometimes that is an expression of joyous affection and even pride; at other times it's the expression of a somewhat different sentiment. I always know which sentiment she is expressing by the context in which she says it. In a similar way, there is much of the Bible that we can properly understand only when we "hear" it in the context in which it was originally written.

We are concerned here primarily with the New Testament. None of the New Testament was written in the context of twentieth-century America. It was all written during the first and early part of the second centuries when the Roman Empire was young and vital and ambitious and when Christianity was a very small minority religion struggling for acceptance and identity. If we are to understand rightly what the New Testament says, we must "hear" it in the context in which it was written.

Finally, to listen to the Bible means that we must learn to recognize and accept the writers' ways of expressing themselves. All parents of teenagers are well aware of the fact that different generations have different ways of expressing what they have to say. The New Testament speaks to us across the span of almost twenty centuries. Modern translations have performed a tremendous service by bringing the Bible into modern languages and expressions. However, there are limits to how far translators can go in modernizing biblical expressions without modifying the biblical message. In studying the Bible, we do well to use at least two, and preferably more, modern translations or versions and to stay alert for the original meanings which the writers themselves were trying to convey.

It's also important to remember while studying the Bible that the real truth about the character of God and the meaning of human life was made known in the world through an historical process and the people who lived it. That process involved, primarily, the Israelites and reached its consummating fulfillment in the life and work of one Jesus of Nazareth, who was God's Messiah, or Christ. Let's repeat that. The real truth about the character of God and the meaning of human life was made known in the world through an historical process and the people who lived it. That process involved, primarily, the Israelites and reached its consummating fulfillment in the life and work of one Jesus of Nazareth, who was God's Messiah, or Christ.

The Bible is the written record of how the people who lived it understood their experiences of that historical process. The authority of the Bible is based upon the truth of that which the writers were experiencing and writing about.

That should be so obvious that no reminder is needed. However, somewhere along the way, many of us have allowed a runaway reverence for the Bible to mesmerize us into the belief that the truth was made known *in* the writing of the record. We cut ourselves off from the possibility of a full and proper understanding because we confuse the vehicle that records the reception of the message with the message itself. We have made the Bible into an idol, and all too often our study of the Bible is idolatry. Children who rush into the street to meet the ice-cream wagon know the difference between the ice cream and the wagon. Christians who study the Bible should know the difference between the truth and the vehicle that conveys the truth.

Perhaps it is appropriate to sound a warning to those who are eager to get on with the business of applying the truth that was in Christ to the problems of life today. Before we can apply the truth that was in Christ, we must know what that truth really was; and before we can know what it really was, we must know the real Jesus who had it and demonstrated it for all the world for all time. It is in the Jesus of there and then that we encounter the Christ for here and now.

We should also be forewarned that we can, and almost surely will, miss the whole point of everything if we try to find specific biblical solutions to modern problems. If we aren't careful, we'll find ourselves searching for scriptural Band-Aids to cover up surface symptoms when the real message is a prescription for radical surgery. The real truth that was in Christ is not merely a collection of shrewd gimmicks to solve everyday problems; it is a whole new way of life, a new way of ordering life, a new way of seeing life and the world around us. The heavenly Father that we meet and come to know in Christ is not an indulgent granddaddy patching up our broken toys; he is an infinitely compassionate Creator who rearranges our inner values and fills our lives, when we let him, with the moral and spiritual power to overcome and conquer problems. How he does that is the message of the New Testament. That's the truth that the writers had experienced and that they are trying to share with us through their writings.

During the almost twenty centuries that it has been in existence, the New Testament has been regarded by Christians as the authoritative guide to the Way in which the world can be saved from sin and death. The writers personally witnessed and experienced that Way in the person of Jesus Christ. They preserve their understanding of that Way for us and share it with us in their writings. When we learn the New Testament, we learn what God is really like and what humans are supposed to be like.

2
Rules for Understanding the Bible

Dismiss the idea that you cannot understand the Bible. While it is true that there are portions and facets of the Bible that no one can ever completely understand, the important message of the Bible can be understood by anyone who can read.

Dismiss the idea that there is a quick-and-easy, foolproof way to understand the Bible. The Bible is a very big book containing the most important message ever heard in the world: the real truth about the character of God and the meaning of human life. It is unrealistic to expect that we can achieve a full and proper understanding of that message by merely reading a few preselected verses at the breakfast table or before going to bed at night.

Study large portions rather than just a chapter or verse at a time. The shorter portions may be all right for personal devotions or special reference, but truly to understand the Bible in depth, a person must read and study it as it was meant to be read and studied: book by book. (It would be interesting to know how many of the preachers who lead chapter-by-chapter or verse-by-verse Bible studies would be willing for their congregations to hear or study their sermons paragraph by paragraph or sentence by sentence. That's not the way to understand the real message. On the contrary, that's the way to misunderstand.)

Reserve sizable blocks of time for Bible study. For a serious study of something as big and important as the Bible, one full, uninterrupted, undivided hour per week should be considered the minimum. Two such hour-long periods would be better. An hour per day would be better still. For most people, an early morning hour is ordinarily the best.

Read each book or combination of books being studied as a unit from at least two different translations or versions. The additional insights gained from reading different versions make this a most worthwhile investment of time. After all, we aren't trying to see how much we can read; we're trying to see how much we can understand.

Get some help, but not too much. Give due consideration to different opinions and interpretations, but read it for yourself and trust your own ability to understand what you read.

Keep a notebook handy and make notes of whatever you feel would be beneficial to you and your study of the Bible. You might find it helpful to make your own detailed outline of the contents of each book. You should, of course, underline or otherwise mark appropriate passages in your Bible. And don't hesitate to make notes in the margins.

Watch for things that are lifted up and expressly emphasized as important. Too often we scarcely notice things the Bible presents as very important, and instead we emphasize things it merely mentions in passing. This may be a necessary and permissible practice for understanding historical and geographical references and descriptions, but it is neither necessary nor permissible for determining the real message the writers were trying to convey.

Don't look for hidden or special meanings or messages. The Bible was written for the purpose of communicating the tremendously important truth that the writers had seen, heard, and experienced. Some were better writers than others, but all of them were trying their best to make readers understand what they had to say. While there is often more truth in a statement than is obvious at first reading, we should be extremely cautious about finding any meaning or message other than that which the writers were clearly trying to convey. Perhaps the most prevalent mistake made in studying the Bible is that of reading into it ideas and meanings which are not really there.

Don't waste a lot of time on things you cannot understand. Concentrate time and attention on things that are easily understood. Many people bog down early in Bible study because they spend too much time and effort trying to understand the "ununderstandable." If you encounter something that just doesn't make sense to you, read it again and consult a commentary; and if it still doesn't make sense, forget it and move on. One word of caution: don't hide from hard sayings by pretending not to understand. It's easy to understand what Jesus meant when he said, "Love your enemies." The difficulty is in doing it!

Don't try to make any single verse, statement, parable, or whatever into the complete, final, and absolute truth. As everyone knows, a biblical text can be found to "prove" almost anything anyone wishes to prove. That is the wrong way to use the Bible. If you are really serious about learning the Bible, study the whole thing; then form your understanding of individual pieces (verses, statements, parables, whatever) in the light of the whole thing.

Guard against the danger of making the Bible your idol and Bible study your whole religion. It's very important, though sometimes difficult, to remember that there's no particular credit in merely studying the Bible, or even in understanding it. The credit comes when we become who and what we are supposed to be.

Keep the character of Jesus Christ at the center of your understanding of the entire Bible. He is the Truth personified. He wrapped up all the real truth the Israelites had been struggling to grasp throughout the Old Testament and demonstrated it for all the world for all time. The New Testament is the written record of how the earliest Christians, some of them eyewitnesses, understood their experiences of Jesus and his significance for their lives. While the entire Bible is essential for the full and proper understanding of Christ, a knowledgeable understanding of Christ is essential for the full and proper understanding of the entire Bible.

Be in an open, receptive, prayerful attitude; but don't let a runaway reverence for sacred Scripture blind you to the very

simple, straightforward, down-to-earth message that the Bible is trying to convey. Don't bring a lot of your own questions. The Bible does not tell us, not even in some secret, spiritual code, everything we would like to know; but it tells us everything we need to know about the character of God and the meaning of human life. It is the written record of how the real truth about God and human life came to be known in the world. Accept the Bible for what it is, and eventually everything will begin to fit together in a big picture that shows what God is really like and how we humans can become what we are supposed to be.

When you have worked your way through the Bible, start over and do it all again. The second, and each succeeding, study is even more exciting, more beneficial, more enlightening than the one before. We never learn it all!

3
The Writing of
the New Testament

Before all the writings included in the New Testament were completed, the church, or the early Christian fellowship, had experienced five more or less distinct stages of development. By familiarizing ourselves with those five stages and the writings which were produced during each, we are better able to understand what the writers were really trying to say and why they said it as they did.

The reader should be aware that the early church did not always move from one stage to the next as abruptly as this brief summary may seem to imply. While there was a somewhat abrupt change from what we are calling the first stage to the second, the later changes were much more gradual, with each stage lapping over into both the one preceding it and the one that came after.

The reader should also be aware that there is wide disagreement among Bible scholars concerning the particular stage in which certain New Testament books appeared. I have tried throughout this study to work around the scholarly debates and controversies as much as possible and simply present the position that I believe is most likely to be accurate. When there is a serious question about the origin of any given book, I have tried to remember to mention it in the introductory comments and notes on that book. However, there is little or no disagreement concerning the general conditions which faced Christians during the period of time when the New Testament was being written. Our primary interest in this chapter is to familiarize ourselves with those general conditions.

Christ's Life and Ministry

The first stage in the development of the church was Christ's earthly life and ministry, including his death and resurrection. The Four Gospels—Mark, Matthew, Luke, and John—provide the record of this stage, although they were actually written during later stages.

As long as Jesus was physically present, the "church" was merely a movement within Judaism. It was composed of Jesus and his followers. The only organization was the appointment of twelve apostles with Jesus as their leader and Judas, apparently, as their treasurer. Some of the twelve were more aggressive leaders than others, but there was nothing comparable to the institutionalized organization that was to come later.

The message proclaimed during this stage consisted of the teachings of Jesus himself. His teachings amounted to a stirring call for radical compassion and sacrificial service toward others. The kind of compassion and service Jesus called for was based upon humble repentance and total devotion to God and his kingdom. "If any man would come after me, let him deny himself and take up his cross and follow me. For whoever would save his life will lose it; and whoever loses his life for my sake and the gospel's will save it" (Mark 8:34b-35). That theme was often repeated and was always involved in everything he taught.

Jesus encountered growing opposition from the Jewish leaders because they saw in him and his teachings a threat to their religion and religious institutions. Eventually, they succeeded in having him executed. This threw his followers into a state of utter despair. They had hoped that Jesus was the long-awaited Messiah, but their hopes died with Jesus on the cross. Their despair changed to ecstatic joy and relief when they learned, and were convinced, that he had risen from the dead. Those who were convinced that he had risen gathered themselves together to wait for whatever was to come next. What came next was the Pentecost experience, and that ushered in the second stage of the church's development.

Persecution by Jewish Officials

After the crucifixion and resurrection, the followers of Jesus no longer had his physical presence to lead them and teach them. Instead, they had the apostles and an unquenchable belief that Jesus had risen from the dead and was still with them as the Holy Spirit. Their experience at Pentecost with its spectacular outpouring of the Holy Spirit is often considered the birthday of the church.

The Jewish officials who had tried to destroy Jesus now found themselves confronted by a growing number of Jews who not only believed but also were persuading others to believe that the Jesus who was crucified was the risen Christ. It's not surprising that the Jewish officials made a strong effort to silence the early Christians. The result was a serious and permanent split within Judaism between those who believed and those who did not believe that Jesus was the Christ, or Messiah.

This was a time of heroic faith and witness by the apostles and other Christians who were drawn together by their belief in Jesus. The sometimes fierce opposition of nonbelievers drove them into a very close and strong fellowship. For a time, they brought all their possessions together in a kind of communistic arrangement as they clung to their belief and waited for Christ to return and complete his triumph on earth. That communistic arrangement didn't last very long, but it represented the first organization of the fellowship that was to become the institutional church.

None of the New Testament was written in its present form during this stage, but the message being proclaimed was preserved and is recorded in the form of the sermons found in the first part of the Acts of the Apostles. (Note especially Peter's sermon on the day of Pentecost, Acts 2:14-36.)

This second stage was an age of pure evangelism. The main problem was persuading other Jews to believe that Jesus was their Messiah. The essence of the apostles' message was that God had raised Jesus, who had been crucified, from the dead and that everyone who repented and believed would be saved and would receive the Holy Spirit as promised by the prophets.

But then Saul of Tarsus became the apostle Paul, and another problem arose, pushing the young church into its next stage of development.

Controversies with Jewish Christians

When Barnabas and Saul began their missionary work, they envisioned it as merely an extension of evangelism among the Jews in other lands. Everywhere they went, they entered the synagogue and tried to convince the Jews that Jesus was their Messiah. But the Jews in those synagogues in other lands, with few exceptions, were not convinced. Barnabas and Saul—it very quickly became Paul and Barnabas—were regularly thrown out of the synagogues they entered. The Jews would not believe; so Paul and Barnabas began telling Gentiles about Jesus. And many of the Gentiles believed! Paul and Barnabas returned from their first missionary journey with glowing reports of the door God had opened for the gospel among the Gentiles.

But, alas, every silver lining has a cloud! The Jewish Christians—many of them anyway—insisted that these Gentile converts who were accepting the Jewish Messiah would also have to accept the Jewish laws, including circumcision. According to this view, all Gentiles could become Christians, but they had to become Jews first. Paul vigorously objected to that. This was the first really big controversy in the young church; and a general church convention, or conference, was called to resolve it.

Actually, that conference didn't really resolve the controversy, although it did reach a formal and official conclusion that was meant to resolve it. The conference was held in Jerusalem with James, the Lord's brother, presiding. (It's reported in Acts 15.) The apostles and elders were gathered for the occasion. Peter made a speech in support of the Gentiles, and Barnabas and Paul reported on their success among the Gentiles. Then James suggested what seemed to him to be the proper way to resolve the problem. The delegates to the conference promptly adopted his suggestion.

The details of their decision were put in a formal communiqué and sent out by formal couriers under the authority and auspices of "the brethren, both the apostles and the elders, to the brethren who are of the Gentiles in Antioch and Syria and Cilicia . . ." (Acts 15:23). The full communiqué is recorded in Acts 15:23-29.

This general conference of the church leaders is significant because it shows that the church had become something more than a mere fellowship of believers; it was well on its way to becoming an independent, institutionalized organization with its own rules and regulations and membership requirements. The maverick movement within Judaism was becoming a separate religious institution with its own distinctive message and mission in the world.

Not everyone agreed with the decision of that Jerusalem conference. The problem still was not really resolved. Many Jewish Christians continued to insist that the Gentile converts should be circumcised and required to observe all the Jewish laws. These "Judaizers" were the ones who created the problem that Paul was so upset about and dealt with in his letter to the Galatians. We also catch glimpses of his conflicts with the Judaizers in his correspondence with the Thessalonians, Corinthians, and Philippians. It was under the pressure of this controversy that he developed his message of salvation through faith rather than by works of the law. He explained his views on that subject in some detail in his letter to the Romans.

During the previous stage, the main message had been designed to persuade Jews that Jesus was their long-awaited Messiah. During this stage, the main message was represented by Paul's insistence that the one and only thing required of everyone, Jew and Gentile alike, was a trusting faith in Jesus Christ who was more than just the Jewish Messiah; he was the Savior Christ for the whole world. This was not a new message, but it was a new emphasis that came to the top during this time of controversy with Jewish Christians who insisted that in order for Gentiles to become Christians, they had to become Jews.

Paul was the leader among those who made full use of the door God had opened for the gospel among the Gentiles. Eventually, Gentile converts began to outnumber Jewish Christians in more and more churches. This created another problem and ushered in the fourth stage of development for the church.

Instability of Gentile Christians

By the time the church entered its fourth stage of development, the rate of growth among the Jews had slackened. Just about all the Jews who could be persuaded to believe in Jesus as the Christ had already been persuaded. Although the church at Jerusalem continued to be considered the mother church for quite some time, the real action was out on the mission field in Asia Minor and Europe where Gentiles were coming into the fellowship in large numbers.

The problem was that these Gentile converts were coming into the church from pagan and heathen backgrounds, and they were bringing many of their former beliefs and practices with them. They were making a mistake similar to that of the Judaizers who had tried simply to add to Judaism a belief in Jesus as the Christ. It would be an overstatement to say that these Gentile converts simply added a belief in Jesus as the Christ to their former religions, but they did bring some of the beliefs and practices of their former religions and tried to assimilate these into the church. Some of these beliefs and practices were quite immoral.

Obviously, there was a great need for some genuine Christian education among the Gentile converts. This may be one of the reasons why a major portion of the New Testament came to be written during this stage. (Another reason was that the church was expanding over such a wide area that written messages were often the only way Christians could communicate with one another. Also, and perhaps most significant, this was the period during which many of the apostles and other eyewitnesses died, thus creating a need for some permanent record of the things they had taught.)

The question of the relationship between Gentile converts and their former religions—and their families, friends, and associates who still worshiped according to their former religions—was the basic problem that prompted Paul's correspondence with the Corinthians, Colossians, and perhaps Ephesians. The Letter of James, which stressed the high moral standard of the

Christian life, was also probably addressed to this problem. Other New Testament books written during this period included at least three of the Gospels (Mark, Luke, and Matthew) along with Acts, Hebrews, and First Peter.

First Peter was written in response to a particular situation. In the year A.D. 64, while Nero was emperor, a great fire burned much of the city of Rome. Nero placed the blame for that fire upon the Christians—who were innocent, incidentally—causing them to be severely persecuted. According to tradition, both Peter and Paul were martyred during this persecution. However, before he was killed, Peter wrote a letter to his fellow Christians in an outlying region of the empire, warning them of the persecution that would soon reach them and encouraging them to "do right and entrust their souls to a faithful Creator" (1 Peter 4:19).

The main emphasis in the message being proclaimed during this stage was that Christianity is the one true religion; Jesus Christ—or Christ Jesus as they often called him—is the sole and sufficient Savior for anyone and everyone who accepts him and follows him. Included in that message emphasis was the insistence that the Christian life is different from other lives.

It was during this stage that a subtle change began to take place in the meaning conveyed by the word "faith." Paul, in his earlier letters anyway, used the word "faith" to refer to a radical, trusting confidence in God and Christ that resulted in the total commitment or surrender of one's whole self. But later, when pagan and heathen beliefs were competing for acceptance in the church, faith began to refer to believing the right (Christian) doctrines. This first change in the meaning of the word "faith" was the prelude of the next stage in the development of the church.

Heresy Challenges True Faith

It was inevitable that eventually one or more of the foreign beliefs or practices which crept into the church amid the influx of Gentile converts would gain enough strength to challenge seriously the supremacy of genuine Christianity. When it finally happened, the church entered its fifth stage of development, and it was during this stage that the last books to be included in the New Testament were written.

The main challenging heresy is known as Gnosticism. The Gnostics taught that salvation depended upon—or consisted of—possession of a special kind of spiritual knowledge or wisdom. The Greek word for this knowledge or wisdom was "gnosis," which is how the heresy got its name. According to the Gnostics, this gnosis was a special gift from God that was bestowed upon only a favored few. The Gnostics, of course, believed that they were the favored few. They believed that they were the only ones who "knew the truth" or "walked in the light," and everyone else was doomed regardless of what they believed or did.

Another Gnostic teaching that genuine Christians considered especially abhorrent was that Christ did not really become truly and completely human; he only "seemed" to be human, and he only "seemed" to suffer and die. The Gnostics had so completely spiritualized Christ that the physical Jesus was largely ignored. The writer of John's Gospel was thinking of Gnosticism when he wrote in his prologue, "In the beginning was the Word, and the Word was with God, and the Word was God. . . . And the Word became flesh and dwelt among us . . ." (John 1:1, 14). The Gnostics believed that "the Word" was too purely spiritual ever to become actually entangled with flesh.

Many Gnostics put their teachings together in such a way as to convince themselves that they were somehow above such earthly things as human morality and decency. They believed they could do as they pleased because they had the gnosis; they were enlightened; they knew the truth. According to that view, human morality and ethics were for the poor unfortunates who were not so favored.

The most direct and outright Christian attack against this heresy is contained in the three letters of John. He was referring specifically to the Gnostics when he said, "For many deceivers have gone out into the world, men who will not acknowledge the coming of Jesus Christ in the flesh . . ." (2 John, v. 7). In another place, he attacked the most basic Gnostic teaching when he said, "God is love, and he who abides in love abides in God, and God abides in him" (1 John 4:16b). John was saying that the distinguishing mark of a true Christian is not the possession of the gnosis; rather, it is love for the brethren. In still another place he says, "He who says he is in the light and hates his brother is in the darkness still" (1 John 2:9). So much for those who believe they are above morality because they claim to have some special knowledge or wisdom!

In addition to John's Gospel and three letters, other New Testament books written during this stage were First and Second Timothy, Titus, Jude, the Revelation to John, and Second Peter. The main purpose of these books, with one exception, was to rid the church of the false teachings and doctrines of the Gnostics and restore allegiance to the true teachings and doctrines of the original apostles, including Paul. There may have been other heresies in the church at the time, but Gnosticism was the strongest and most influential. Gnosticism was so strong and had such a large following that it came treacherously close to replacing the true message and mission of the Christian faith and way. That's why the Christian writers during this stage were so vigorous in their call for people to take a firm stand for the accepted faith of the established church.

The one exception was the Revelation to John, which was a response to another severe Roman persecution of Christians, this time under the emperor Domitian. The Gnostic heresy was not totally ignored in the vision John reports in Revelation, but the main purpose and message concerned the significance and ultimate outcome of the Roman persecution.

Another possible exception was the Gospel According to John, which obviously had a bigger and broader purpose than merely combating a particular heresy. However, it is just as obvious to the careful reader that the writer of John's Gospel had this heresy in mind and wrote his account of the life and teachings of Jesus in such a way as to provide a strong proclamation of Christian truth in opposition to Gnosticism.

Modern Bible students and scholars sometimes take a condescending attitude toward some of the writings which appeared during this stage of the church's development because so much emphasis is placed upon the acceptance of established beliefs and doctrines. This extreme "doctrinalism," so noticeable in First and Second Timothy, Titus, Jude, and Second Peter, seems—and is—far removed from the simple teachings of Jesus. However, it is very important for us to remember why Christian writers during this stage emphasized right doctrine so strongly. If they had not done so, Gnosticism with its wrong doctrines would have overwhelmed the church and Christianity would have become a distorted caricature of the powerful and redeeming influence it was meant to be.

The church has passed through many stages of development since the completion of all the writings included in the New Testament. Each stage has been characterized by adaptation of the main emphasis in its message to the particular conditions and situation of its own time. When it has been at its best, the church has based its message emphasis firmly and solidly upon the foundation that was laid by the lives and teachings of Jesus Christ and his apostles and other eyewitnesses. When the church has gotten away from that foundation, it has become something other than what it is supposed to be. The only way we can be sure that we are on that foundation is by constantly, seriously, prayerfully, and intelligently studying the written record prepared by those who were actually there and who helped lay that foundation. That written record is our New Testament.

Simplified Summary of the New Testament Era.

Approximate Date	General Situation	Emphasis of Message	Status of the Church	New Testament Writings
28	Christ's Life and Ministry. Christ's Ministry Crucifixion	"Deny self, follow me, seek first the kingdom of God." We had thought he was the Messiah. Despair.	Growing band of tentative followers of Jesus.	(Recorded in Gospels, but they were written later.)
30	Resurrection	He is the Messiah!	Ecstatic joy and relief.	
	Persecution by Jewish Officials. Split within Judaism between those who believed and those who did not believe Jesus was the Messiah.	The Messiah has come! Jesus rose from death and lives. God's Holy Spirit is with us. Repent and be saved.	Informal fellowship of believers. Sharing together and waiting for Christ to return in complete triumph.	(Sermons by apostles in Acts.)
45	Controversies with Jewish Christians.	Salvation by faith, not observance of law. Life in the Holy Spirit sets all persons free from sin and death.	Organization formalized. Leaders make decisions for entire fellowship. Independent institution and religion.	1 & 2 Thessaloni- ans Galatians 1 & 2 Corinthians Romans
60	Instability of Gentile Christians. Brought in pagan belief and practice (belief in many spirits, sexual immorality). Roman persecution.	Christ is sole and sufficient Savior. Christian life is different from other lives. Stand firm and trust.	Organization refined. ("Bishops" appear as apostles die). Faith begins to change to believing right doctrines. Gospels written to preserve stories of Jesus' life and to instruct Gentiles.	Colossians Philemon Philippians Ephesians James 1 Peter Hebrews Mark Luke Acts Matthew
90	Heresy challenges true faith. Paganisms consolidate. Gnosticism leads many astray. Second severe Roman persecution.	Stand firm for original beliefs. Remember what apostles taught. False beliefs destroy chance for salvation.	Seriously split by strong heresy. True believers rally to defend the faith. Stressed loyalty to the "accepted faith" and to the established church. Began collecting Paul's letters and "other scripture."	1, 2, & 3 John 1 & 2 Timothy Titus Revelation John Jude 2 Peter

Section 2
"The Things Which Have Been Accomplished Among Us"

Inasmuch as many have undertaken to compile a narrative of the things which have been accomplished among us, just as they were delivered to us by those who from the beginning were eyewitnesses and ministers of the word, it seemed good to me also, having followed all things closely for some time past, to write an orderly account for you, most excellent Theophilus, that you may know the truth concerning the things of which you have been informed.

Luke 1:1-4

4
The Gospel According to Mark

Author: John Mark, an associate of Peter (1 Peter 5:13) and of Paul

Date: Sometime between A.D. 60 and 70

Place: Probably in Rome

Theme: Jesus, a great wonder-worker among the people, was the long-awaited Messiah whom the religious authorities opposed and condemned to death.

Mark portrays Jesus as a man of action, a great wonder-worker who was always in a hurry. Christ's teachings play a relatively minor role in this Gospel. It's almost as though he had so much to do before he was to be betrayed and crucified that he didn't have time to preach or teach. Notice how often Mark uses the word "immediately." (The King James Version translates this word as "straightway.") This mood of great urgency to be going places and doing things is particularly noticeable when you read straight through the Gospel—as it was meant to be read—rather than when you stop after every chapter.

It's also interesting to note the prominence Mark gives to the personal opposition and persecution Jesus faced throughout his ministry. It begins in the second chapter, and by the third chapter his enemies are conspiring to destroy him (3:6). The shadow of the cross hangs very heavily over this entire Gospel. Six of the sixteen chapters are devoted to the last week of Jesus' earthly life, the period during which he was betrayed and crucified.

This Gospel was written for people living in an age of crisis. During the time Mark was writing this Gospel, Rome, under Emperor Nero, was severely persecuting Christians. Some were even being hunted down and killed. According to tradition, it was during this persecution that both Peter and Paul were martyred. John Mark, the author of this Gospel, had been a missionary companion to Paul, Barnabas, and Peter (Acts 12:25; Colossians 4:10; 1 Peter 5:13). After Peter was killed, Mark wrote this Gospel to preserve the memory of the things Peter had told about Jesus.

It might be expected that Mark, writing against that background, would present Rome in the role of the villain. However, he doesn't. Mark makes it very clear that the Jewish authorities, rather than the Romans, were responsible for the persecution and death of Jesus. Moreover, it was one of Jesus' own chosen apostles who betrayed him, and it was none other than the great apostle Peter who denied that he even knew Jesus. This account of Peter's denial of Jesus is especially interesting because Peter was Mark's main source of information for this Gospel. Mark records several interesting and undoubtedly embarrassing incidents which Peter apparently told on himself.

It's also noteworthy that, according to Mark, Jesus tried to keep secret his identity as the Messiah, especially during the early part of his ministry. This same kind of secrecy is also noticeable in the Gospels of Matthew and Luke, both of which used Mark's Gospel as the basic outline for their own accounts. This contrasts sharply with the Gospel According to John in which Jesus is reported to have claimed openly from the beginning that he was the Messiah. Usually, Jesus seemed to prefer the phrase "Son of man," although in John he sometimes called himself the "Son of God." There are subtle differences in the meanings of the two phrases, but the reader is safe in understanding them to mean essentially the same thing when Jesus used them to refer to himself.

Although at the time Mark was written much of the remainder of the New Testament had already been written, this is the first of the Four Gospels to be written. Mark was probably in Rome when Peter was martyred, and he wrote this Gospel soon thereafter. The original ending has been lost. Different endings following Mark 16:8 appear on various early manuscripts. It is very uncertain how Mark's original ending was lost. It was probably accidentally torn off the original scroll before scribes started making copies for distribution to different churches. Different scribes then added an ending to the incomplete scroll from other sources of information available to them.

Outline
(two sittings suggested to read the entire book)

Sitting One: I. Introduction and Preparation for Ministry (1:1-13)

                II. Ministry in and Around Galilee (1:14-9:50)

Sitting Two: III. Journey to Jerusalem (10:1-52)

                IV. The Last Week (Chapters 11-15)

                V. The Empty Tomb (16:1-8)

                VI. He Lives!—Various Endings (16:9-)

5
The Gospel According to Matthew

Author: An anonymous Jewish Christian using the Gospel of
Mark and a collection of Jesus' teachings compiled
by Matthew
Date: About A.D. 85
Place: Antioch in Syria (?)
Theme: The Messiah, Jesus, was a great teacher who suffered,
died, and was raised from death in fulfillment of the
old law and the prophets to become the Savior for the
whole world.

Anyone who desires to sit "at the feet of the Master" and listen
to him talk about God and the true meaning of human life should
devote much time and careful attention to the Gospel According to
Matthew. While it doesn't contain all his teachings, Matthew
contains more of Jesus' teachings than any other book in the Bible.

It's in this Gospel that we find the famous Sermon on the
Mount (chapters 5-7) which is almost universally accepted as the
classic description of the Christian life. That sermon should be
studied in its entirety carefully and often. Most of the problems

which plague most of our lives most of the time would disappear if we lived by the teachings contained in that sermon.

Other important groupings of teachings by Jesus found in Matthew include his instruction to his disciples (chapter 10), parables of the kingdom (chapter 13), instructions concerning certain personal and community relationships (chapter 18), severe condemnation of Pharisaic piety (chapter 23), and a discussion of the last days (chapters 24-25).

Matthew is the only Gospel that specifically mentions the church (16:18 and 18:17). In addition to those two specific references, certain parables seem to assume that the church is the visible, earthly manifestation of the kingdom of heaven. Incidentally, the other Gospels use the phrase "kingdom of God" where Matthew uses "kingdom of heaven." Both phrases refer to the same thing.

While the writer obviously had a very high regard for the church in the world, his Gospel contains some very emphatic warnings against the danger of trusting too much in institutionalized religion. The woes to the Pharisees and scribes in chapter 23 and much of the Sermon on the Mount in chapters 5-7 make it clear that Jesus is not at all impressed—perhaps we should say that he is impressed the wrong way—by a pious show of religion or attachment to empty religious forms and institutions. Jesus is far more concerned about the genuine inner person than he is about any outward appearances.

By the time this Gospel was written, the church included large numbers of Gentiles who had been converted directly to Christianity. This created the very important and controversial question of the relationship of Gentile Christians to the old Jewish laws. We will study that controversy in more detail when we get to the book of Acts and the letters of Paul, but notice here how Matthew combines and reconciles the interests of both Gentile and Jewish Christians. He repeatedly emphasizes the universal, worldwide mission of Jesus and his church, but he also bends over backward to show that Jesus fulfilled the Jewish law and prophets —even to the point of reporting that Jesus entered Jerusalem sitting on two donkeys! (See 21:4-7.)

Matthew plays upon the theme of the fulfillment of prophecy

almost to the point of monotony. The writer was very obviously well acquainted with the Old Testament (Jewish Scripture), and he referred to it over and over in order to show that the things Jesus did and said fulfilled the role of the Messiah whom God had promised through the prophets. The writer, along with the writers of the other three Gospels, was not so much interested in merely informing his readers about the facts of Jesus' life as he was in showing his readers that the facts of Jesus' life proved that he was the Messiah.

Apparently, the writers of both Matthew and Luke had copies of Mark's Gospel. Both of them reproduced almost all of Mark, some of it word for word. In addition, the Gospels of Matthew and Luke contain significant amounts of other material that is so similar that it seems to have come from another source that they also had in common. This has led scholars to theorize that there was another document, referred to as "Q," which consisted primarily of the teachings of Jesus (since that is what the similar material in Matthew and Luke consists of) and that both writers used "Q" as well as the Gospel of Mark as their sources.

There is additional evidence for the existence of such a document in a book written about A.D. 140 by a bishop of the church named Papias in which he said, "Matthew composed the sayings (of Jesus) in the Hebrew language, but everyone interpreted them as he was able." Some, but not all, scholars believe that this collection of sayings composed by Matthew was the "Q" document. If it was, then the apostle's work provided an essential part of the core of this Gospel that bears his name.

It is extremely unlikely that the apostle Matthew himself could have written this Gospel in its present form. For one thing, there is nothing outside the title to indicate that the apostle wrote it. On the contrary, it depends heavily upon Mark, which indicates that the writer was not an eyewitness but, rather, someone who brought together information from different sources which he considered reliable. He recorded what eyewitnesses reported.

Whoever the writer was, he performed a tremendously significant and beneficial service for all subsequent Christians. By the end of the second century, Christian writers were quoting this Gospel more frequently than any other book in the New Testament.

That's probably true of modern Christian writers as well. The nineteenth-century French scholar Renan called Matthew "the most important book in the world." Very few Christian people would argue with that evaluation.

Outline
(three sittings suggested to read the entire book)

Sitting One:

I. Genealogy and Birth of Jesus (Chapters 1-2)
II. Preparation and Preaching
  A. Baptism and Temptation (Chapters 3-4)
  B. Sermon on the Mount (Chapters 5-7)

Sitting Two:

III. Gaining Popularity
  A. Series of Miracles (Chapters 8-9)
  B. Instructions to Disciples (Chapter 10)
IV. Resistance and Opposition
  A. Questions and Controversies (Chapters 11-12)
  B. Parables of the Kingdom (13:1-52)
V. Recognition as the Christ
  A. Conflicts, Peter's Confession, Transfiguration (13:53-17:27)

Sitting Three:

  B. Teachings on Human Relationships (Chapter 18)
VI. Christ Arrives in Jerusalem
  A. Journey to Jerusalem (Chapters 19-22)
  B. Woes to Pharisees (Chapter 23)
  C. Teachings About the Last Days (Chapters 24-25)
VII. Passion, Death, and Resurrection (Chapters 26-28)

6
The Gospel According to Luke

Author: Luke, the beloved physician and companion of Paul and of Peter
Date: A.D. 75–80
Place: Rome (?)
Theme: Jesus was the Savior Christ for all people; Gospel shows special concern for the sick, the poor, and the outcasts.

Luke was a Gentile writing to and for other Gentiles. He also wrote the Acts of the Apostles, which picks up where his Gospel leaves off. (Compare Luke 1:1-4 with Acts 1:1-2.) He wrote both the Gospel and Acts after Paul had established that Gentiles could become Christians without becoming Jews.

Compared to the other Gospels, Luke reports very little activity and teaching of Jesus which apply specifically to Jewish practices. It omits the story of the Gentile woman whose request Jesus was reluctant to grant (Mark 7:24-30 and Matthew 15:21-28). It does not suggest, as does Matthew, that Jesus wanted the Jews to be given priority in hearing the gospel (see Matthew 10:5-6).

Instead, Luke includes some new parables, teachings, and activities of Jesus which show as much concern for Gentiles as for Jews. Luke is the only Gospel that reports the parables of the good Samaritan and of the prodigal son.

Luke seemed concerned to show that there was no real conflict between Christianity and Rome. Time and again, throughout both his Gospel and the book of Acts, Luke reported that the Roman officials failed to find anything offensive in Jesus, Christians, or Christianity. For Luke, the real conflict was with the Jewish leaders, not Rome.

The possibility has been suggested that Luke was trying to convince Rome that Christians were entirely separate and distinct from the Jews who had openly rebelled against Rome a few years earlier and who were still often guilty of civil disobedience. It's as though Luke were trying to show "Theophilus" (1:3) that while the Jews were the bad guys, Christians were among the good guys. If Theophilus was a Roman official, as is commonly supposed, this possibility edges toward probability. ("Theophilus" is a Greek word meaning "friend of God." Luke could have been using it as simply a way of addressing his Gospel and Acts to all Christians. More likely, however, Theophilus was the name of a Roman official.)

Luke was a good writer. As he points out in his introduction (1:1-4), he researched his subject very thoroughly and relied upon a number of sources. In the discussion of Matthew, we noted that two of those sources were Mark and the "Q" document. Luke edited these sources and added large amounts of other material not included anywhere else. The result is the most smoothly written, easily read, and happiest of the four Gospels.

Luke soft-pedals the suffering and agony that is portrayed so vividly in the other Gospels. For example, Matthew's account of the birth of Jesus ends with the infant being smuggled out of the country to avoid the general massacre of all male children; Luke's account ends with the infant being carried to the temple where he is recognized and worshiped as the hope of the world, "a light for revelation to the Gentiles, and for glory to thy people Israel" (2:32). Luke makes the shadow of the cross seem less ominous and Christ's suffering less intense than do the writers of the other Gospels.

This Gospel shows a strong sympathy for the underprivileged and social outcasts. For example, Matthew's first beatitude says, "Blessed are the poor in spirit . . ." (Matthew 5:3); Luke says simply, "Blessed are you poor . . ." (6:20). Also, Luke seems to show an even more special concern for Samaritans than the other Gospels. All the Gospels, indeed all the writings in the New Testament, reflect a special concern that Jesus felt for the sick, the poor, and the outcasts; but this concern is lifted up more clearly in Luke than elsewhere.

Other interesting emphases to be found in Luke are the frequency of reports that Jesus withdrew from the crowd to pray and the prominent role of women in his life and work. Luke also emphasized the workings of the Holy Spirit. This Spirit emphasis is even more noticeable in Luke's second book, Acts.

Outline
(three sittings suggested to read the entire book)

Sitting One: I. Birth and Childhood of Jesus (Chapters 1-2)

II. Preparation for Ministry (3:1-4:13)

III. Ministry in Galilee (4:14-9:50)

Sitting Two: IV. Journey to Jerusalem (9:51-19:44)

Sitting Three: V. Passion, Death, and Resurrection (19:45-24:53)

7
The Gospel According to John

Author: Anonymous disciple of the apostle John
Date: A.D. 95–100
Place: Jerusalem or Ephesus (?)
Theme: Jesus was the eternal God in physical human form, bringing God's loving mercy and abundant life to all who would receive him.

This Gospel, more than any of the others, takes us inside the mind of Jesus. It has been said that the other Gospels "give us Jesus as he was known to others whereas John gives us Jesus as he was known to himself." While the other Gospels emphasize "the things which have been accomplished among us" (Luke 1:1*b*), John is more concerned with the spiritual meaning and significance of those things. This is not to suggest that John is less reliable than the others in reporting historical events (sometimes he is probably more reliable); rather, this suggests that John had a different perspective or purpose for writing. Compare John 20:30-31 with Luke 1:1-4.

It is doubtful that the apostle John actually wrote this Gospel, but it is very probable that he was the major source of information for the writer. It is generally believed, although not certain, that John was the "beloved disciple" (or merely "the disciple") who is so prominent in this Gospel. That "beloved disciple" was almost surely the major source of information for chapters 13–20. Only someone who was a very close associate and confidant of Jesus could have known—or would have dared even to try imagining—so much of what Jesus himself thought and felt during that part of his ministry.

In contrast to the other three Gospels, John reports that Jesus openly proclaimed that he was the Messiah from the beginning of his ministry. Also in John, the cleansing of the temple is placed at the beginning of his ministry rather than at the end. John does not mention the baptism, temptation, transfiguration, or the agony in Gethsemane. The other Gospels strongly suggest that Jesus' ministry covered only one year (one Passover mentioned); John suggests a ministry of three years (three Passovers mentioned). John reports Jesus in Jerusalem several times, whereas the others place him there, as an adult, only once. John introduces new characters, such as Nicodemus and the woman of Samaria, and adds the miraculous raising of Lazarus as one of the most important and crucial acts of Jesus' ministry.

These and other differences make John's Gospel stand apart from the Synoptic Gospels (Matthew, Mark, and Luke) and create insurmountable difficulties for anyone who tries to reconstruct a precisely accurate account of Jesus' historical ministry. But these differences also serve to remind us that none of the Gospel writers thought of himself as writing what we call a biography. They were not especially interested in recording a precisely accurate account of the life of Jesus. Rather, they were listing the historical evidence to support their deep, personal conviction that Jesus was the Christ.

The prologue (1:1-18) is perhaps the most beautiful and profound statement of who and what Jesus Christ was and why he was here that has ever been written. It is not easy to understand. It may even be impossible to understand completely, but the truth expressed in those verses is the very heart of the Christian faith.

Notice Jesus' growing anguish at the approach of "the hour"

for which purpose he came. John apparently understands the crucifixion as the focal point of all human history.

Chapter 17 is a long prayer by Jesus as he looks back at his earthly ministry and forward to the cross and his return to his Father in heaven. Notice especially how he includes you and me in that prayer.

As you read chapters 18 and 19, try to imagine yourself in Pilate's place with his responsibilities, both to Rome (whose occupation forces he represented) and to the Jews (with whom he was supposed to maintain friendly and peaceful relations), and ask yourself if you could have done any better, or even as well!

There is an abrupt change of mood, style, and feeling at the beginning of chapter 21. Perhaps the notes or report by the "beloved disciple" ended with chapter 20, and the writer added other information he had at hand.

There are several abrupt changes of mood or subject, and even the location of Jesus, scattered through this Gospel. Some scholars believe that the writer was using notes which had been written at different times and that when writing this Gospel, he put some of those notes in the wrong places.

Outline
(two sittings suggested to read the entire book)

Sitting One: I. Prologue (1:1-18)
                 II. Preparations (1:19-51)
                 III. Early Ministry (Chapters 2-6)
                 IV. Growing Opposition and Conflict (Chapters 7-12)

Sitting Two: V. Preparing Apostles for "the Hour" (Chapters 13-17)
                 VI. Betrayal, Trial, and Crucifixion (Chapters 18-19)
                 VII. Resurrection (Chapters 20-21)

8
The Acts
of the Apostles

Author: Luke, the physician
Date: A.D. 75-80
Place: Rome (?)
Theme: Experiences, activities, and teachings of Christ's followers after his death and resurrection

This is the only record of its kind in existence that tells the story of the origin and early development of the Christian church. Acts is the sequel to the Gospels in general and Luke in particular. The author, Luke, begins Acts where he ended his Gospel. He wrote this second volume to inform "Theophilus" (whoever that was) about the true meaning and significance of "the things which have been accomplished among us" (Luke 1:1*b*), this time by the apostles, especially Peter and Paul.

Acts is an extremely important book because of the history it records, but we miss its major importance if we regard it as pure history. Luke, like other Bible writers, was not simply recording history; he was *using* history to prove the validity and redeeming power of the Christian faith and way.

51

The emphasis on the workings of the Holy Spirit that was noticeable in Luke's Gospel is present again in Acts. The apostles and other early Christians were very keenly aware of the power, presence, and guidance of the Holy Spirit in everything they did.

Chapter 2 records the beginning of the church as a church. That's the chapter that tells about Pentecost and the famous and spectacular outpouring of the Holy Spirit. Notice, however, that the outpouring of the Holy Spirit, in and of itself, created only amazement, perplexity, and mocking accusations that the Christians were drunk. The good stuff didn't start happening until "Peter, standing with the eleven, lifted up his voice and addressed them" (Acts 2:14) with the first recorded Christian sermon following the crucifixion and resurrection. Study Peter's sermon (2:14-36) very carefully. This is the message the early Christians proclaimed to the world. This is the message that converted three thousand people that day and brought the Christian church into being. When we think of that Pentecost experience, it's all too easy to get so carried away with the spectacular that we miss the significant.

There are several sermons recorded in Acts. Even though they are almost surely summaries of the actual sermons preached by the apostles, they are very significant because they reveal the Christian message as it was proclaimed by the earliest Christians.

Chapter 6 records the beginning of the church bureaucracy. A problem arose in the fellowship; so a committee was appointed. Notice that they appointed laymen so that the apostles could be free to devote themselves "to prayer and to the ministry of the word."

Chapter 15 reports the first general church convention, or conference. A serious controversy was building; so spokesmen for both sides were called to Jerusalem to work out their differences. James, the brother of Jesus, was the moderator. He was apparently the head of the church in Jerusalem, and the church in Jerusalem was apparently the head church of the world at that time. The apostle Paul was very much involved in that controversy, and an understanding of that council or conference will be very beneficial when we study some of his letters.

Certain sections of Acts were written in the first person. These are commonly referred to as the "we" sections because Luke tells where "we" went and what "we" did. These sections were apparently copied from a personal diary or journal that Luke kept while traveling with Paul. He was an actual eyewitness to the events reported in these "we" sections.

Special values of Acts include a report of what happened to Christ's followers after his death and resurrection. It explains how the Christian church came into being and what it considered its main message and mission in the world. And Acts tells us who the man was who wrote a bunch of letters to a bunch of churches and signed them with the name "Paul."

Outline
(three sittings suggested to read the entire book)

Sitting One:
    I. Church Beginnings in Jerusalem (1:1–6:7)
    II. The Church Expands Through Palestine (6:8–9:31)

Sitting Two:
    III. The Church Expands into Syria (9:32–12:25)
    IV. The Church Expands into Asia Minor (13:1–16:5)
    V. The Church Expands into Europe (16:6–19:20)

Sitting Three:
    VI. The Church Reaches Rome (19:21–28:31)

Section 3
Letters of
the Apostle Paul

*Paul, a servant of Jesus Christ,
called to be an apostle, set apart for
the gospel of God. . . . To all
God's beloved . . . who are called to
be saints: Grace to you and peace
from God our Father and the
Lord Jesus Christ.*

Romans 1:1-7

9
First and Second Thessalonians

Author: Paul
Date: About A.D. 50
Place: From Corinth
Theme: Reassurance and exhortations concerning Christian belief and conduct while waiting for Christ to return

Many believe that First Thessalonians was the earliest of the New Testament books to be written. If so, Second Thessalonians, which followed soon after, was the second. Paul wrote these letters to a church that he had founded. Read Acts 17:1-15 for a report of Paul's experiences in Thessalonica. He encountered some fierce opposition from the Jews while he was there. So fierce was the opposition that he was slipped out of town by night and sent to Beroea. He stayed in Beroea for a while; then, leaving Silas and Timothy at Beroea, he went to Athens. After a brief stay in Athens, he went to Corinth where Silas and Timothy rejoined him. He was in trouble with the Jews in Corinth, but he stayed there eighteen months. (The "Silas" in Acts is apparently the "Silvanus" in the salutation of Paul's letters.)

Meanwhile, he worried about the Christians in Thessalonica. He had been forced to leave town hurriedly, and it is very natural that he would be anxious about what was happening in his absence. So he sent Timothy to find out. When Timothy reported back to him, Paul was tremendously relieved, and he sat down and wrote his first letter.

First Thessalonians

The first three chapters are almost mushy with lavish expressions of joy and thanksgiving that the Thessalonians were holding together so well and witnessing so powerfully under some very trying circumstances. The Thessalonian Christians, most of whom were Gentile converts (see Acts 17:4), were being persecuted by their fellow Gentiles in much the same way that Jewish Christians were being persecuted by their fellow Jews (1 Thessalonians 2:14). Paul was very proud of the Thessalonians, and he told them so.

However, after he bragged on them for three chapters, he issued a mild reprimand by reminding them of what he had taught them about sexual morality while he was there. This was quite a problem for many Gentile converts because their former religions often had a very freewheeling attitude toward sex. Paul very gently but firmly reminded them that things were different now that they were Christians.

Then, after bragging on them some more for their love for the brethren, he got to a question that was disturbing the Thessalonians themselves: what happens to those who die before Jesus returns? Apparently, they had not understood his teachings on that matter while he was with them. In this letter he tried to clear it up. But, alas, they misunderstood him again!

Second Thessalonians

Somehow, sometime after Paul sent the Thessalonians his first letter, he learned that they were still confused about when the Lord is going to return. That's the main subject of his second letter. In this letter he warned them "not to be quickly shaken in mind or excited, either by spirit or by word, or by letter purporting to be from us, to the effect that the day of the Lord has come" (2:2). It seems that one reason he was having so much difficulty clearing up this point was that someone kept feeding them various theories and interpretations and even kept writing letters and signing Paul's name. It's interesting to note that there were already controversies in the church when the New Testament was just beginning to be written. It's also interesting and significant to note that there was letters "purporting" to be from Paul but which obviously were not.

Give special attention to what he says about the "coming of the Lord" and the "day of the Lord" and about the "man of lawlessness" who is to precede that event. Paul explains that the "mystery of lawlessness" is, at that time, already at work but is being temporarily restrained. He had talked to the Thessalonians about this when he was there (2:5). It would be very helpful to us if we knew what he had told them. We will encounter some of these ideas again; so don't settle too firmly into any interpretation yet. Just notice and remember what Paul says here.

Outline
(one sitting suggested to read both books)

First Thessalonians:
    I. Personal Greetings and Thanksgiving (Chapters 1-3)
    II. Special Problems
        A. Warning Against Immorality (4:1-12)
        B. Instructions Concerning the Coming of the Lord (4:13–5:11)
        C. General Instructions (5:12-22)
    III. Conclusion (5:23-28)

Second Thessalonians:
    I. Personal Greetings (Chapter 1)
    II. More Instructions Concerning the Coming of the Lord (2:1-12)
    III. General Instructions (2:13-3:15)
    IV. Benediction and Farewell (3:16-18)

10
Galatians

Author: Paul
Date: A.D. 54 (?)
Place: From Ephesus (?)
Theme: Angry defense of Paul's authority and teachings

Paul wrote this letter in response to a serious controversy in the churches of Galatia concerning the relationship of Gentile Christians to the old Jewish law. He held some very deep convictions on this matter, and they form a major theme throughout his writings; but nowhere does he state his position more forcefully than he does in this letter.

Paul had founded the churches in Galatia during his first missionary campaign (Acts 13:13–14:26). Even then, there had been opposition from the Jews, but the Christian converts, Gentiles and Jews, had accepted with gladness Paul's gospel of grace through faith. Now someone was going around to the churches teaching that Gentiles must become Jews (i.e., be circumcised) before they could become Christians. This was a direct contradiction of what Paul believed and taught, but these new teachers claimed that Paul was not really an apostle since he had not been one of the original Twelve. Therefore, what he believed and taught had no authority. Many of the Galatian Christians believed these new teachers.

In this letter, Paul defended both the authenticity of the gospel he preached and the authenticity of his apostleship. He was hurt and angered by what was happening in the churches, and he didn't waste a lot of time or words trying to be tactful or diplomatic. He just wanted to get this thing straight once and for all; so he said what he had to say as forcefully as he could. He was obviously angry when he wrote this. He may have said more than he should have.

Galatians has been called the Christian declaration of independence. In this letter, Paul set forth the position that resulted in the establishment of Christianity as a separate religion clearly distinguishable from Judaism. A good understanding of what Paul says here will be very beneficial when we study the remainder of his letters, especially those to the Corinthians and to the Romans.

It's very important to notice the particular meaning Paul gives to certain words, such as "faith," "flesh," "spirit," and "freedom." He didn't always mean exactly the same thing we mean today when we use these words.

In the second chapter of this letter, Paul mentions a trip to Jerusalem to discuss with the apostles—James, Peter, and John—the gospel he preached among the Gentiles. The book of Acts reports several of Paul's trips to Jerusalem. It's uncertain which trip Paul refers to here. You might like to compare his account in the second chapter of Galatians with the trips reported in Acts 15:1-29 and 21:15-25. Neither trip fits Paul's description exactly, but they come closer than any other trips reported in Acts. The date and place assigned to this letter (found at the beginning of this chapter) assume that he was referring to the trip described in Acts 15 and that he wrote Galatians during his stay in Ephesus on his third missionary campaign. However, there are still questions surrounding these "facts."

Outline

(one sitting suggested to read the entire book)

I. Defense of Paul's Ministry (Chapters 1-2)

II. Defense of Paul's Gospel (Chapters 3-4)
III. The Morality of Christian Freedom (Chapters 5-6)

11
First Corinthians

Author: Paul
Date: A.D. 54–55
Place: From Ephesus
Theme: Practical advice concerning a number of problems of Christian conduct and relationships within the church

First Corinthians has been called the most typical church letter in history because it opens with a fight over the preacher and closes with a collection. Even if we disregard the fight and collection, we still have a very typical church letter, or at least a letter to a very typical church. There were numerous conflicts, questions, and problems tearing the Corinthian church apart. Paul discusses these conflicts, questions, and problems one at a time, exhorting the Corinthians to be more Christian in their conduct and relationships and then explaining in very practical terms how to do that.

Corinth was the capital of Achaia, a province in Greece. Paul's first stay in Corinth is reported in Acts 18:1-18. (It's not really important, but it's interesting that Sosthenes, the ruler of the Corinthian synagogue, was beaten by the Jews in the presence of Gallio, the Roman proconsul [Acts 18:17]. Then, Sosthenes was with Paul in Ephesus and sent his greetings along with Paul's to the "church of God which is at Corinth" [1 Corinthians 1:1-2]. Was this the same Sosthenes? I rather suspect it was, don't you?)

Corinth was a thriving commercial center, very prosperous and very corrupt. It contained numerous temples to numerous pagan gods, some of which were extremely immoral. Many—perhaps most—of the Corinthian Christians had been converted from these pagan or heathen religions and had grown up in the city where sexual permissiveness was the accepted life-style. This probably accounted for their indifference toward the man living with his father's wife (apparently his widowed stepmother) and for Paul's bitter condemnation of that situation. It was only natural that Paul would react very strongly to any sign that the prevailing immorality was creeping into the Christian church.

The presence of so many pagan temples with their elaborate sacrificial rites probably also accounted for the question concerning food that had been offered to idols. This was undoubtedly a big problem for the Corinthian Christians whose friends, neighbors, and relatives were still worshipers of these pagan gods. Everywhere they went, they were offered food that, in one way or another, had been blessed or dedicated to some pagan idol. Paul talks about this in two places: 8:1-13 and again in 10:14-31. If you read carefully, you will notice that the position he finally comes to is not quite as permissive or tolerant as we have sometimes been led to believe.

This letter was written several years before any of the Gospels. Paul's report of the resurrection of Jesus in 15:3-8 is the earliest written report of the resurrection that we have. Also notice that Paul reports it here as the summary, or reminder, of the gospel he preached to them when he first came to Corinth. This was the gospel that they received, in which they stand, and by which they are saved (15:1-2).

This letter also contains the earliest written account of what happened at the Lord's last supper (11:23-26).

At the beginning of chapter 7, Paul addresses himself to "the matters about which you wrote." Obviously, the Corinthians had

written him for advice and instructions on certain matters. The
first question he deals with concerns marriage. Everything he said
was based upon his belief that the end was very near. Notice verses
26, 29, and 31. If we keep his comments in that context, we discover
that he was not nearly as unrealistic or puritanical as some have
accused him of being. However, when we get to his discussion of
women in the church (11:2-16 and 14:34-35), we find a definite
tendency toward chauvinism as well as a tendency toward the kind
of legalism that he bitterly opposed in other matters.

The most important question he discusses in this letter
concerns the resurrection of the body and the Christian hope for
life everlasting (15:12-58). Belief in a life after death was nothing
new to the Greek converts. The Greeks had long believed in the
immortality of the soul, according to which the soul was
imprisoned in the body until released by death to go off into some
other realm where it became part of a greater or purer reality. That
was not what Paul believed. The opening statement in his
discussion of this question (15:12) indicates that some of the
Corinthian converts had rejected his idea of the resurrection of the
body. Further on into the discussion, it appears that some had
rejected the whole idea of *any* life after death. Study Paul's
discussion of this very carefully.

Undoubtedly, many of the Corinthians scoffed when they read
what is now 6:7-8. Many people still scoff at that. But that's the way
Christianity is supposed to work, and Paul was telling the
Corinthians that Christian people and Christian churches are
supposed to be Christian.

In 5:9, Paul refers to an earlier letter that he had written to the
Corinthians. That earlier letter has been lost. However, it's
possible that a fragment is preserved in 2 Corinthians 6:14-7:1.
That section seems misplaced at that location, and it almost fits the
description of the letter referred to in 1 Corinthians 5:9.

The real heart of this letter, of course, is chapter 13. It's hardly
an overstatement to say that the remainder of this letter is simply
the practical application of the message in that chapter. Notice
that he placed these comments in the very center of his discussion
of spiritual gifts and that he introduced these comments as "a still
more excellent way" (12:31).

Outline

(two sittings suggested to read the entire book)

Sitting One: I. Party Strife and Disunity (Chapters 1-4)

                II. A Case of Immorality (Chapter 5)

              III. Christian Lawsuits in Pagan Courts and the Sanctity of Our Bodies (Chapter 6)

              IV. Marriage (Chapter 7)

                V. Food Offered to Idols (Chapters 8-10)

Sitting Two: VI. The Veiling of Women (11:1-16)

              VII. Observance of the Lord's Supper (11:17-34)

            VIII. Love and Spiritual Gifts (Chapters 12-14)

              IX. Immortality and Resurrection (Chapter 15)

                X. The Collection (Chapter 16)

12
Second Corinthians

Author: Paul
Date: A.D. 55
Place: Ephesus and Macedonia
Theme: Angry defense of Paul's authority, and a tender
rejoicing in reconciliation

Second Corinthians, as it appears in our New Testament,
contains two separate letters. The earlier is preserved in chapters 10
through 13, the latter in chapters 1 though 9.

The church at Corinth caused Paul much trouble and
anguish. In trying to resolve the difficulties he had with this
church, Paul wrote at least four letters. In 1 Corinthians 5:9 he
refers to an even earlier letter than that. We have already noted that
this earlier letter has been lost, with the possible exception of a
fragment that may have somehow been preserved in 2 Corinthians
6:14-7:1. Anyway, the letter we know as First Corinthians was the
second letter Paul wrote to Corinth. The third letter is preserved in
Second Corinthians, chapters 10 through 13, and the fourth letter
in chapters 1 through 9.

As strange as it may seem to us, First Corinthians failed to have any real effect. Indeed, the situation in the church at Corinth continued to grow steadily worse. Not only did the immorality and disunity continue to flourish, but they also seem to have been condoned if not actually encouraged by false teachers whom the Corinthians were following. These false teachers were undermining Paul's influence, attacking his character, and teaching a different version of the gospel than he had taught. Paul never did appreciate that sort of thing!

He made a quick trip to Corinth to try to straighten matters out after First Corinthians failed. He refers to this as a "painful visit" (2 Corinthians 2:1). But this visit didn't do any good either; so he wrote them another (his third) letter. This was a very harsh letter. It was so harsh that, for a time anyway, he regretted having written it (see 2 Corinthians 7:8).

This harsh letter is preserved in chapters 10 through 13. In it, Paul attacks head-on the false teachers who had led the Corinthians to fall away from their original allegiance to the gospel he had preached to them. The insistence that all Christians observe Jewish laws, including circumcision, was involved, but the more serious problem seems to have been the factionalism that Paul had talked about at the beginning of First Corinthians. The factionalism that had disturbed him earlier had become an open conflict between numerous personality cults. The leaders of these cults had ganged up on Paul and were accusing him of being weak, an unskilled speaker, crafty, and probably an embezzler of the funds he had collected in the churches. These are some of the specific charges he answers in 2 Corinthians 10–13.

It is important to remember that it was in the context of answering such charges that Paul indulged in what he admitted were foolish boasts of his own sacrifices and accomplishments on behalf of Christ. He was saying, in effect, that if the Corinthians were looking for the teacher with the most spectacular credentials, he would gladly match his credentials with anybody. Notice in 11:16-33 all the things Paul had endured, but notice also how strongly he emphasized the foolishness of boasting about such things. Even in all his anger and bitterness, and in spite of all the sarcasm he put into this letter, he somehow managed to keep himself in perspective and to keep Christ at the center. The more carefully you study this letter, the more obvious it becomes that Paul was not trying to reassert himself as the dominant leader of the church as much as he was trying to call the Corinthians back to a genuine allegiance to the real Jesus Christ.

After sending Titus to deliver this harsh letter to the Corinthians, Paul became impatient to learn what the effect would be. This is probably when he had the second thoughts about some of the things he had written. He was so anxious about it that he passed up an opportunity at Troas to preach the gospel in order to go into Macedonia and meet Titus returning with word from Corinth (2:12-13).

Titus reported that the harsh letter had caused the Corinthians to repent, reject the false teachers, and renew their loyalty to Paul's gospel. Their rejection of at least one false teacher was so severe that Paul would caution them in his next letter to go easy with him (2:6-8). It was there in Macedonia, after learning the good results of the harsh letter, that Paul wrote his fourth letter to Corinth, the letter of grateful reconciliation that is preserved in 2 Corinthians 1-9.

There is a very noticeable contrast of mood between this letter of reconciliation and the harsh letter. His bitterness has turned to affection; his anger has turned to gratitude; his sarcasm has turned to confident praise. Even if we knew nothing else about his relationship with this church than what we read in these nine chapters, we could recognize that Paul was writing in an attitude of grateful relief that a very difficult conflict had been resolved. Notice especially how he explains the resolution of the conflict in terms of reconciliation with God: "Therefore, if any one is in Christ, he is a new creation; the old has passed away, behold, the new has come. All this is from God, who through Christ reconciled us to himself and gave us the ministry of reconciliation; that is, in Christ God was reconciling the world to himself, not counting their trespasses against them, and entrusting to us the message of reconciliation. So we are ambassadors for Christ, God making his appeal through us. We beseech you on behalf of Christ, be reconciled to God" (5:17-20).

He includes a brief discussion of eternal life. In First

Corinthians he seemed to be saying that those who die must wait for a general resurrection when everybody will receive a new "spiritual body" and will enter into the eternal life with God in Christ. Here, he seems to be saying that everything is already prepared and waiting for us and that we enter into the eternal life at the moment of death. In fact, we are already entering it. ". . . Though our outer nature is wasting away, our inner nature is being renewed every day" (4:16).

He closes with an appeal for the collection. Apparently, the Corinthians had stopped gathering the collection when the controversy became heated. Now Paul appeals to them "to complete what a year ago [they] began not only to do but to desire" (8:10). It's interesting to note that he uses the generosity of the Macedonians to spur the Corinthians to greater generosity but then goes on to explain that he had used the Corinthians as an example to spur the Macedonians.

Perhaps it should be pointed out that the visit he threatened in 12:14-13:10 was delayed, as he explains in 1:23-2:1. However, he did visit Corinth again after he wrote the letter of reconciliation; while he was there, he wrote his letter to the Romans.

Outline

(two sittings suggested to read the entire book)

Sitting One: I. The Harsh Letter
        A. Paul's Sincerity (10:1-11:6)
        B. His Self-Support (11:7-15)
        C. Sufferings for the Gospel (11:16-12:13)
        D. The Threatened Visit (12:14-13:10)
        E. Salutation and Benediction (13:11-14)

Sitting Two: II. The Letter of Reconciliation
        A. Salutation and Thanksgiving (1:1-11)
        B. Review of Strained Relationship (1:12-2:17)
        C. Vindication of Paul's Apostleship (3:1-6:13)

D. Marriage with Unbelievers (6:14–7:1)

E. Appeal for Complete Reconciliation (7:2-16)

F. The Collection (Chapters 8-9)

13
Romans

Author: Paul
Date: A.D. 56
Place: From Corinth
Theme: Humble, trusting faith in Christ Jesus brings deliverance from sin and death and is the genuinely meaningful way of living.

Shortly after completing his correspondence with the Corinthians, Paul arrived in Corinth and spent some time there (Acts 20:1-3). It was during this stay in Corinth that he wrote to the Romans. This was soon after the controversies and conflicts in Corinth and Galatia had been resolved. Probably one of the main reasons he wrote this long and carefully worded letter to the Romans was to head off similar controversies and conflicts in the church at Rome. He wanted to present his version of the gospel to the Christians in Rome before someone else got to them with a different version. Since it would be some time before he could visit them in person, he wrote this letter, the most comprehensive and systematic presentation of Paul's message that we have.

Romans is not an easy letter for us to understand, but it is more than worth the effort to try. It concerns the deepest and most basic questions of the Christian faith and life. In this letter, Paul uses certain words and discusses certain ideas which seem very familiar—justification, righteousness, faith, flesh, sin, freedom, and others—but when Paul uses these words, he does not always mean the same thing that these words have come to mean for many later Christians. The key to understanding Romans is to understand what Paul meant when he used these words and discussed these ideas. We must let Paul speak his message in his own way rather than read our own message into what he was saying.

In the first section (chapters 1-8) he talks about salvation. Perhaps the three most important words or ideas which appear in this section are "righteousness," "justification," and "faith."

For Paul, righteousness does not mean merely being morally good. It's not something we humans can simply grit our teeth and do or accomplish. For Paul, righteousness refers to "The Right" or "The Truth" that ultimately and inevitably prevails. The God of creation is altogether good, and his way is always the right way, and when everything has happened that is going to happen, God and his "righteousness" will be triumphant. In Christ we can share in that righteousness, but we cannot produce it ourselves. It is God's righteousness, and its triumph depends entirely upon God and his activity.

Likewise, justification depends upon God rather than upon anything we can do or accomplish. We cannot justify ourselves by obeying laws or being religious or anything else. For Paul, there is something wrong with humans, beginning with Adam, that makes it impossible for us to be what we are supposed to be. Paul uses his personal experience to illustrate the universal human experience when he says, "So I find it to be a law that when I want to do right, evil lies close at hand . . . making me captive to the law of sin . . ." (Romans 7:21-23). He was saying that it is in our human nature to be sinners. There is nothing we can do to justify ourselves before God as long as we are bound to our sinful human nature. Paul cries out in desperate anguish, "Wretched man that I am! Who will deliver me from this body of death?" (7:24). Then he

comes right back with a cry of joyous relief, "Thanks b
through Jesus Christ our Lord!" (7:25a). He is saying th
through Christ, releases us from bondage to our nature. W.   .we
turn our whole selves over to Christ and when his Spirit fills our
whole being, we are set free from sin and death. "There is therefore
now no condemnation for those who are in Christ Jesus. For the
law of the Spirit of life in Christ Jesus has set me free from the law
of sin and death" (8:1-2).

Salvation is made effective through faith; and when Paul
speaks of faith, he does not mean believing in Christian doctrines,
although that is involved; rather, he means entrusting our total
selves to Christ. For Paul, faith means putting our old self
completely behind us—he calls it dying to our old self—so that
Christ can bring us to new life in his Spirit. "For if we have been
united with him in a death like his, we shall certainly be united
with him in a resurrection like his. We know that our old self was
crucified with him so that the sinful body might be destroyed, and
we might no longer be enslaved to sin" (6:5-6). It was Paul's
message that we receive the gifts of God's grace when we turn our
backs upon our own ways and our own schemes and our own
efforts and give ourselves completely to Christ and life in his Spirit.
This is what Paul means by faith.

In chapter 8, Paul brings all this together in a very powerful
summary and concludes this section of the letter with a strong
affirmation of his faith that nothing "in all creation, will be able to
separate us from the love of God in Christ Jesus our Lord" (8:39).

In the second section of the letter (chapters 9-11) he deals at
some length with the problem of why the Jews—many of them
anyway—reject Jesus as the Messiah. It must have been very
confusing to the Gentiles who were being asked to believe that
Jesus was the Jewish Messiah to see so many Jews rejecting him.
Paul tries to clear up this question in this section of his letter, and
in the process he says some very important things about faith and
about God's love for all peoples.

The third section (chapters 12-15) is devoted to the description
of the Christian life. Paul is not content merely to explain
Christian doctrine; he proceeds to make a very practical
application of doctrine to everyday life.

Chapter 12 deserves special mention here and special attention in any New Testament study. It ranks just behind Christ's Sermon on the Mount as a practical statement of what it means to live the Christian life.

Chapter 16 is a personal note and was almost surely written at another time and place and intended for the church at Ephesus. There are any number of ways it could have been attached to the end of the letter to the Romans.

Outline
(two sittings suggested to read the entire book)

Sitting One:

I. Salvation by Grace Through Faith in Christ
   A. Gentiles Separated from God (Chapter 1)
   B. Jews Separated from God (Chapter 2)
   C. Faith Brings Both to God (Chapter 3)
   D. Abraham's Example as Proof (Chapter 4)
   E. Christ Undoes the Sin of Adam (Chapter 5)
   F. Christ Frees Us from Sin (Chapter 6)
   G. Christ Frees Us from the Law (Chapter 7)
   H. Benefits of Life in Christ (Chapter 8)

Sitting Two:

II. Problem of the Rejecting Jew (Chapters 9-11)
III. The Christian Life
   A. A New Mind in Christ (Chapter 12)
   B. Christians and the State (13:1-7)
   C. Love and Light (13:8-14)
   D. The Strong and the Weak (Chapters 14-15)
IV. Note to the Ephesians (Chapter 16)

14
Colossians and Philemon

Author: Paul
Date: A.D. 61–63
Place: From a Roman prison (?)
Theme: Jesus Christ is the all-sufficient Savior and Guide for personal religion and relationships.

Paul's letter to the Colossians was a general letter to the church and was intended for public reading (Colossians 4:16). It was Paul's response to a serious heresy that was gaining momentum in the Colossian church. The same, or similar, heresy spread to other cities and troubled Christians for quite some time. In fact, some elements of that heresy still linger in some churches even today.

The letter to Philemon ("and Apphia our sister and Archippus our fellow soldier, and the church in your house"—v. 2) was a personal note from the apostle to an individual slaveholder who was a member of the Colossian church. This letter was an appeal to that slaveholder on behalf of a runaway slave. We are combining the letters to the Colossians and to Philemon into one study unit because they are both very short and because they were both written at the same time and delivered by the same messengers to the same town. That was not mere coincidence. There is a subtle but significant relationship between these two letters that is part of the evidence for a tremendously fascinating theory concerning the fate of that runaway slave.

Colossae was located about one hundred miles east of Ephesus. It was not a very significant town in the political or commercial affairs of that time. Paul apparently never visited Colossae. The church there was founded by Epaphras, a friend and associate of Paul. It was Epaphras who brought word to Paul that Christianity at Colossae was assimilating—or being assimilated into—the popular but pagan religions of the area. Paul was in prison when he received that word and when he wrote these two letters. It could have been during a time of imprisonment in Ephesus, or in Caesarea, or in Rome. Rome seems more likely.

There is some uncertainty about the precise beliefs and practices of the pagan religions which were making inroads into Christianity at Colossae. The particular form Paul was reacting to seems to have been a combination of many religions, including Judaism. The result of this combination of religions was a special type of mystery religion that sought release from the evils of the material world by worshiping a hierarchy of spiritual forces which, supposedly, control access to God. One of the problems was that the Colossians were trying to include Christ as one of those spiritual forces. They were simply making room, as it were, for Christ in their pagan religions. In response to that, Paul emphasized as strongly as he could the full sufficiency of Jesus Christ: "For in him the whole fulness of deity dwells bodily, and you have come to fulness of life in him, who is the head of all rule and authority" (2:9-10).

The Colossian paganism also tried to influence the spiritual forces and win favor with God by observing religious festivals and seasons and sabbaths, by worshiping angels, by following special visions, and by submitting to numerous regulations (2:16-22). Paul says, "These have indeed an appearance of wisdom in promoting rigor of devotion and self-abasement and severity to the body, but they are of no value in checking the indulgence of the flesh" (2:23).

In Colossians, Paul reacts to "super piety" that tries to make Christianity into a system of doctrinal or philosophical beliefs and/or religious rules, regulations, and rituals. For Paul, Christianity is a new life in Christ, "in whom are hid all the treasures of wisdom and knowledge" (2:3). He is telling the Colossians that Jesus Christ is fully sufficient and that they should look to him, and him alone, for salvation.

Having made that as clear as he could, he proceeds—as was his usual practice—to describe the practical application of the new life in Christ. In chapter 3 and part of chapter 4, he discusses the Christian way of living, contrasting the Christian life with the non-Christian life.

Notice in 4:7-9 that Paul is sending word about his personal affairs by Tychicus "and with him Onesimus, the faithful and beloved brother, who is one of yourselves." The Onesimus referred to here was the runaway slave whom Paul was sending back to his master. Along with this letter to the church, Tychicus and Onesimus also brought a letter to the master from whom Onesimus had run away. That slavemaster was a member of the Colossian church, and this reference to the slave was Paul's way of securing the church's support for his plea on behalf of that slave. The owner could have legally executed Onesimus for running away, but Paul was pleading for Onesimus to be received by his owner "no longer as a slave but more than a slave, as a beloved brother . . ." (Philemon, v. 16). The reference to Onesimus in the letter to the Colossians was the public announcement of the personal plea Paul makes in his letter to Philemon.

A careful reading of the first two verses of Philemon leaves a question concerning precisely who owned Onesimus. It could have been Archippus instead of Philemon. If so, the reference in Colossians 4:17 was another and even more direct appeal to the church for support of Paul's plea on behalf of the returned slave.

A more important question raised by a careful reading of the entire letter to Philemon (only twenty-five verses) concerns the precise content of Paul's plea. In the main part of the letter, he stops just short of actually requesting Philemon (or whoever was the owner of the slave) to release Onesimus and send him back to Paul. He says, "I am sending him back to you, sending my very heart. I would have been glad to keep him with me, in order that he might serve me on your behalf during my imprisonment for the gospel; but I preferred to do nothing without your consent in order that your goodness might not be by compulsion but of your own free will" (v. 12-14). He offers to pay the owner for any wrong or any expense the slave has caused and then refers to the tremendous debt the owner owes to Paul: ". . . to say nothing of your owing me even your own self" (v. 19). Finally, in summing up his plea, Paul says, ". . . I write to you, knowing that you will do even more than I say" (v. 21).

It seems obvious that Paul wanted Onesimus freed and returned to him. We are nowhere told what happened to Onesimus, but the fact that this letter was preserved is some evidence that Paul's plea was granted. If it had not been granted, the slave owner would probably have destroyed this letter.

Now consider this: scattered bits of circumstantial evidence from a number of sources point to the fascinating possibility that Onesimus was released by his Colossian owner, that he subsequently rejoined and remained with Paul until Paul was tried and executed, that he then returned to Asia Minor where he eventually became the bishop of Ephesus, and that he was responsible for the first effort to bring together a collection of Paul's letters, thus beginning the process of putting together the New Testament. This theory cannot be proven, but there is a sizable amount of rather impressive circumstantial evidence to support it. For a detailed examination of that evidence, see *The Interpreter's Bible*, volume 11, pages 555-560.

Outline

(one sitting suggested to read both books)

Colossians: I. Greetings (1:1-14)
               II. Full Sufficiency and Supremacy of Christ (1:15-2:7)
               III. Adequacy of Faith (2:8-23)
               IV. New Life in Christ (3:1-4:6)
               V. Further Greetings and Salutation (4:7-18)

Philemon: I. Greetings (vv.1-3)

II. Gratitude for Philemon and Others (vv. 4-7)
III. Plea for Onesimus (vv. 8-22)
IV. Further Greetings and Benediction (vv. 23-25)

15
Philippians

Author: Paul
Date: A.D. 62-64
Place: From a Roman prison
Theme: The richness of the Christian faith and life, discussed in the light of Paul's awareness of his approaching death

Paul was nearing the end of his life when he wrote this letter to his favorite church. He had first visited Philippi in response to the famous vision in which a man said to him, "Come over to Macedonia and help us" (see Acts 16:9). This was during his second missionary campaign, and his relatively brief but very eventful first visit to the city is described in Acts 16:9-40. That description of Paul's experiences in Philippi reveals several very interesting things.

First, this is the beginning of one of the "we" sections of the book of Acts. The writer (Luke) says that when Paul had seen the vision appealing for help, ". . . immediately *we* sought to go on into Macedonia, concluding that God had called *us* to preach the gospel to them" (Acts 16:10, italics added). He continues to describe events in the first person until Paul and Silas are thrown into jail on the charge of disturbing the peace. They had cured the girl who had "a spirit of divination." It is logical to assume that we have an eyewitness account of this visit.

There was apparently no Jewish synagogue in Philippi. Luke says, "And on the sabbath day we went outside the gate to the riverside, where we supposed there was a place of prayer; and we sat down and spoke to the women who had come together" (Acts 16:13). The absence of an established synagogue explains why there was no Jewish opposition to Paul during this visit.

The course of events while Paul was in Philippi contributed to his success in winning converts. The girl with "a spirit of divination" followed him around announcing that he was a servant of God who proclaimed the way of salvation. It may be questionable that many people believed her witness, but she at least brought attention to Paul and what he was saying. Then, the earthquake that came that night while Paul and Silas sat in jail praying and singing hymns was instrumental in effecting the conversion of the jailer and his household. And, finally, the official stir when the magistrates and police discovered that Paul was a Roman citizen whom they had beaten and imprisoned illegally served to make him something of an heroic martyr and made the city feel indebted to him for the injustice that had been done. Even though he was asked to leave town, he went out with dignity and with the respect of the people, and he left behind the makings of a strong and loyal church.

About ten years later, while imprisoned in Rome awaiting trial and probable execution, Paul wrote the Philippians, "I thank my God in all my remembrance of you" (Philippians 1:3).

This is a strange letter in many ways. It has been called a missionary letter because it includes an expression of deep gratitude for the missionary help that the Philippians had provided Paul in various times of need, including his current imprisonment in Rome. However, to classify this as a missionary letter is misleading. There were several other things which concerned Paul as much as, if not more than, the missionary help he had received from the Philippians. (Incidentally, Paul made it a rule to support himself without any help from the churches he founded, but he made an exception to that rule and accepted help from the Philippians while he was in Thessalonica and again while imprisoned in Rome.) It has also been said that the theme of this letter is Christian joy.

While the theme of Christian joy and rejoicing is very obvious in much of the letter, we miss some of the most important things Paul says if we try to make all of it into an expression of joy. There is also a melancholy theme and even a flash of anger.

This letter is best thought of as simply the outpouring of Paul's heart and soul to some very dear friends who had been loyal and helpful throughout his ministry and whom he loved very much. In the church there were no really big problems which he felt compelled to address head-on. There was some petty bickering: a few Jewish Christians were still talking about the necessity of circumcision and the observance of Jewish laws, and there seemed to be some problem of self-righteousness and pride; but the church was apparently handling these things rather adequately all by itself.

Paul wrote this letter late in his ministry, and he used the occasion to share with some very dear Christian friends some of the things which were important to him. While it is not as systematic or thorough as his letter to the Romans, Philippians is a statement of Paul's theology and outlook on life—and death. In prison and awaiting the trial that might very possibly result in the death sentence, Paul here summed up for his friends his own personal feelings and faith.

Notice that he still expected Christ to return, but that expectation no longer involved the sense of urgent immediacy which it did in his earlier letter. By this time, Paul had become aware that Christ's return might be delayed for quite some time.

Philippians contains several favorite and familiar quotations. Great care should be taken to prevent our familiarity with these quotations from obscuring the meaning of what Paul is really saying. Unless we are careful, we will read this letter as though it were merely a collection of famous quotations. It was never meant to be that. It just happens to be a letter in which Paul says a lot of important things.

Outline

(one sitting suggested to read the entire book)

 I. Personal Greetings and Thanksgiving (1:1-11)
 II. Imprisonment and Suffering Serves to Spread the Gospel (1:12-30)
 III. Importance and Nature of True Humility (2:1-18)
 IV. Personal Matters (2:19-3:1)
 V. False Teachers and Paul's Personal Testimony (3:2-4:1)
 VI. A Case of Petty Bickering (4:2-3)
 VII. Final Appeal and Benediction (4:4-23)

16
Ephesians

Author: Paul (?)
Date: A.D. 62-64 (?)
Place: From a Roman prison (?)
Theme: Through his church, Jesus Christ is binding all peoples into a glorious unity.

As we have already discovered, Paul was the leader in the movement that opened the way for Gentiles to become Christians without first becoming Jews. By the time this letter was written, that movement had won the day, and Gentiles were entering directly into the Christian church with very little, if any, opposition from Jewish Christians who had earlier insisted that all Christians must observe Jewish laws. This letter ignores political, racial, social differences and recognizes only two categories of people: Gentiles and Jews. The church is represented as the meeting ground where these two categories of people are brought together in Christ according to God's plan. This plan is referred to as "the mystery of Christ, which was not made known to the sons of men in other generations as it has now been revealed to his holy apostles and prophets by the Spirit; that is, how the Gentiles are fellow heirs, members of the same body, and partakers of the promise in Christ Jesus through the gospel" (3:4-6).

The key words and ideas used to develop the major theme of Ephesians are taken from Paul's earlier letters. Ephesians seems to be a kind of summary of Paul's teachings that was put together as a tribute to the victory of the Christian church that had won its independence from Judaism. We should be very cautious, however, in regarding this letter as a straight summary of Paul's teachings. There is a noticeable tendency throughout to give subtle modifications to his ideas in order to strengthen the emphasis upon the importance of the institutional church.

For an illustration of this tendency, compare Ephesians 2:20-22 with 1 Corinthians 3:5-17. While there is no irreconcilable conflict between these two passages, there is definitely a difference in their meanings and emphases.

It is also worth noting that the idea that Christ would return soon is completely missing from Ephesians. Instead of looking forward to the Lord's return to wrap up history and gather his followers unto himself in heaven, as Paul had done in earlier letters, Ephesians looks forward to the continuing growth and maturation of the church (see 4:11-16). It might also be worthy of note that the idea of Christ descending "into the lower parts of the earth" (see 4:9-10) is not mentioned in any of his other letters.

These and similar modifications of Paul's earlier ideas and insights are among several bits of evidence that convince many Bible scholars that Paul did not write this letter. There is a widely held belief that it was written by a devoted follower of Paul, possibly to serve as the introduction to the original collection of his letters. If so, then it must be considered at least possible that the former slave, Onesimus, was the author. (See comments in chapter 14, "Colossians and Philemon.")

However, there is also evidence that Paul either wrote it or told a "secretary" what to write. Without going into the details of the controversy concerning authorship, since it's not crucial to the understanding of the letter, we will lean toward tradition and give Paul credit, but with a big question mark, for writing it.

There is much evidence and a very widely held belief that it was not written to the Ephesians. It is incredible that Paul, or even someone writing in his name, would have written to Ephesus, where he spent three years and had many close friends, without including personal greetings to a single person. Moreover, he implies that he knew of the readers' faith only by hearsay (1:15) and that they knew of him only by hearsay (3:2). In addition, there is no reference to Ephesus in the body of the earliest manuscripts. The letter was entitled "To the Ephesians," but even the earliest Christian writers argued about whether or not that title was accurate. It's possible that this is the "letter from Laodicea" referred to in Colossians 4:16, but it is almost surely not a letter to Ephesus.

These questions concerning the authorship and destination of the letter also bring into question the date and place of writing. However, none of this should be regarded as a shadow on the authenticity and truth of its message. Regardless of who wrote it or where it was delivered, this document that we know as the Letter of Paul to the Ephesians is a legitimate expression of an extremely important part of the Christian faith and way. Whether it was written by Paul or by one of his devoted followers writing in his name (which, incidentally, was a legitimate and accepted practice in those days), it is a very profound and powerful reminder to all generations that it is God's plan and purpose to bring all peoples together in unity in Christ and that this unity is already being achieved in and through the church.

That theme of unity in Christ is developed in some very beautiful and sublime language in the first three chapters. The last three chapters are devoted to the practical and specific application of that theme to the personal lives of individual Christians.

Outline

(one sitting suggested to read the entire book)

I. Greetings (1:1-2)
II. Unity of All Things in Christ (1:3-3:21)
III. Personal Christian Living (4:1-6:20)
IV. Farewell and Benediction (6:21-24)

Section 4
Letters by Eyewitnesses

Let those who suffer according to
God's will do right and
entrust their souls to a faithful
Creator.

1 Peter 4:19

17
James

Author: James, the brother of Jesus(?)
Date: About A.D. 60 (?)
Place: Jerusalem (?)
Theme: The moral and ethical demands of the Christian
faith and way

This was a general epistle addressed "to the twelve tribes in the Dispersion" (1:1). The literal interpretation of that address would be to all Jews (twelve tribes of Israel) living outside Palestine (in the dispersion). However, the writer almost surely intended it to mean all Christians everywhere. His use of the phrase reflected the belief that Christianity represented the new and true Israel.

Much has been said and written about the origin and authorship of this epistle. Not all scholars agree that James, the brother of Jesus, was the author. James was a very common name, and it could have referred to any number of persons; and the epistle could have been written any time between A.D. 50 and 150. Fortunately, a sure knowledge of who wrote it, or even when it was written, is not necessary to understand what it says.

The purpose of this epistle was to lift up the moral demands of the Christian faith and way. There is very little philosophical theology and doctrine here. The writer seems to have only a minimal concern with purely religious or spiritual matters. Indeed, he says, "Religion that is pure and undefiled before God and the Father is this: to visit orphans and widows in their affliction, and to keep oneself unstained from the world" (1:27). That is reminiscent of the words of the prophet Micah: "What does the Lord require of you but to do justice, and to love kindness, and to walk humbly with your God?" (Micah 6:8); or the words of the prophet Amos: "But let justice roll down like waters, and righteousness like an everflowing stream" (Amos 5:24); or the words of Jesus himself: "Not every one who says to me, 'Lord, Lord,' shall enter the kingdom of heaven, but he who does the will of my Father who is in heaven" (Matthew 7:21).

James has no patience with the idea that being a Christian is merely a matter of believing the right things. To him, being a Christian means *doing* the right things, and that is the general theme of this epistle.

One of the most familiar portions of this epistle is that which discusses the relationship between faith and works. On this point, James seems to be at the opposite extreme from Paul. This is a good place in the study of the New Testament to fix clearly in mind the two different meanings of the word "faith." Compare very carefully James 2:14-26 with Galatians 3:1-14 and Romans 4:1-25. In these passages, James uses the example of Abraham to prove that salvation is by works, and Paul uses the example of Abraham to prove that salvation is by faith. However, if we examine what each of them said very carefully, we discover that the contradiction is not so much in what they were saying as in how they were saying it. The word "faith" meant entirely different things to the two writers.

James, along with some other New Testament writers that we'll study later, used the word "faith" to refer to a set body of doctrinal beliefs. James said that this kind of faith doesn't save anybody. He said, "You believe that God is one; you do well. Even the demons believe—and shudder. Do you want to be shown, you shallow man, that faith apart from works is barren?" (2:19-20).

Paul would have insisted as strongly as James did that this kind of faith is barren or dead. He would also have insisted that this was not the kind of faith he was talking about. For Paul, faith referred to a radical, trusting confidence in the God and Father of Jesus Christ. Paul claimed that when we have that kind of faith, right actions follow; but it is the faith, not the right actions, that brings us into right relations with God.

James also sounds a stern warning for us to be very careful with what we say. ". . . The tongue is an unrighteous world among our members, staining the whole body, setting on fire the cycle of nature, and set on fire by hell" (3:6). There is even more.

He also pronounces a universal condemnation of rich people. He condemns jealousy, anger, grumbling, and favoritism. He warns against taking oaths and calls for prayers, the anointing of the sick, and the confession of sins to one another. And more!

This epistle is a collection of practical moral teachings. It skips and jumps from one subject to another and then back again. It is very disconnected and loosely organized around the general theme that Christians are to behave in accordance with the highest standards of morality and ethics. It makes disturbingly clear how those standards apply to everyday life.

It has been noted that this epistle actually tells us less about Jesus than any other book in the New Testament. There is a theory, with some impressive supporting evidence, that it was originally a Jewish epistle addressed to Jews and that a Christian writer modified it slightly to make it applicable to Christians. Be that as it may, it should also be noted that there are numerous parallels between the teachings of this epistle and the teachings of Jesus in his Sermon on the Mount (Matthew 5-7). Perhaps James tells us more about Jesus than appears obvious at first glance.

Outline

(one sitting suggested to read the entire book)

I. Address and Moral Teachings (1:1-2:13)
II. Faith and Works (2:14-26)
III. Use and Misuse of the Tongue (Chapter 3)
IV. More Moral Teachings (4:1-5:12)
V. Life in the Church (5:13-20)

18
First Peter

Author: The apostle Peter
Date: A.D. 62–64
Place: From Rome
Theme: Encouragement and support for Christians facing persecution and suffering

The Gospels picture Peter as a lovable and loyal but blundering apostle who kept his feet in his mouth much of the time. It was Peter who rebuked Jesus when Jesus revealed his plans to go to Jerusalem to face suffering and death (Mark 8:31-33). It was Peter who drew his sword and attacked the guards whom Judas brought to the garden to arrest Jesus (John 18:10). And who can ever forget that it was Peter who warmed his hands around the fire and denied Jesus in the courtyard of the high priest while Jesus was inside being railroaded to the cross (Mark 14:66-68)!

But now we find Peter writing to his fellow Christians, "Beloved, do not be surprised at the fiery ordeal which comes upon you to prove you, as though something strange were happening to you. But rejoice in so far as you share Christ's sufferings, that you may also rejoice and be glad when his glory is revealed" (4:12-13). Obviously, something tremendous had happened that had brought about a drastic change in Peter. For an explanation of what had happened, see Peter's sermon on the day of Pentecost, Acts 2:14-36, and his prayer in Acts 4:24-30. The new and different Peter who preached that sermon and prayed that prayer is the Peter who wrote this letter.

This was a letter of powerful encouragement to Christians who were, or soon would be, facing persecution because of their faith. It has been described as a letter of hope, but it is important to note that the hope offered here is not the sentimental optimism that everything is going to be all right. Rather, it is religious hope that is rooted in faith (trusting confidence) in the living God who raised Jesus Christ from death and who is holding in heaven for all Christians "an inheritance which is imperishable, undefiled, and unfading" (1:4). The trials and persecutions which were coming to Christians were not things to be merely endured; they were ways to strengthen, prove, and increase the glory of the new life in Christ. Indeed, it was this new life in Christ that received most of Peter's attention in this letter. He describes it in some detail, reminds his readers how far superior it is to their old life, and calls upon them to embrace it with renewed vigor in the midst of their present trials. "Therefore let those who suffer according to God's will do right and entrust their souls to a faithful Creator" (4:19).

An interesting feature of this letter is Peter's claim that Christ descended to the world of the dead and preached to those who had died before his crucifixion in order that they, too, might have the new life. In his letter to the Ephesians, Paul (?) introduced this same idea (Ephesians 4:8-9). Here, Peter refers to it as if it were already an accepted part of Christian belief (3:18-20 and 4:6). It is not known exactly when or how this belief originated, or how widely it was held. It is assumed that the belief represents an effort to explain what Christ was doing between the crucifixion on Friday and the resurrection on Sunday and how salvation was brought to those who died before he came.

Some scholars doubt that the apostle Peter was the author of this letter. They point out that it was about thirty years after Peter was martyred before there was a general persecution of Christians in the area to which this letter was addressed. However, there was a general persecution of Christians in Rome during Peter's lifetime, and it would have been easy for Peter to see the handwriting on the wall, as it were, and know that the persecution would eventually spread throughout the empire. He could have written to prepare the readers for the persecution that would eventually reach them. Indeed, in places he refers to their trials as something in the future. It's easy to understand how he could sometimes lapse into the present tense if he was already experiencing it himself in Rome.

It has also been pointed out that the quality of the Greek in which this letter is written is far above that which is expected from a common fisherman. However, the author explains that he is writing the letter with the assistance of Silvanus (5:12). That's the only explanation necessary to account for the excellency of the Greek. Incidentally, this Silvanus apparently is the Silas referred to in Acts as the occasional companion of Peter and Paul.

Some scholars also claim that this letter does not read as though it was written by a personal eyewitness or associate of Jesus. In contrast, other scholars believe that it reads very much like an eyewitness account by someone who had been with Jesus. In fact, in addition to several claims and implications that he had witnessed certain events in Christ's ministry, the writer seems to have been thinking specifically of the threefold command of Jesus to Peter to "feed [his] lambs" (John 21:15-17) and the foot washing (John 13:5-9) when he wrote 1 Peter 5:1-7. That threefold command and the foot washing were unquestionably more impressive experiences to Peter than to anyone else. Even though it was years later, he was still smarting with the personal significance of those experiences when he wrote this letter.

There are other objections that have been raised to the belief that the apostle wrote this letter, but the weight of evidence strongly suggests that Peter was the author and that he wrote it from Rome during the time when Nero was persecuting the Christians in that city. Many Christians were martyred during that persecution. Among them, according to the best traditions, were Paul and Peter.

It had been a long time and Peter had come a long way since he sat in the courtyard of the high priest and wept at a cock's crowing.

Outline

(one sitting suggested to read the entire book)

I. Salutation (1:1-2)
II. The Blessings of Christians (1:3-2:10)
III. The Duties of Christians (2:11-4:11)
IV. The Trials of Christians (4:12-5:11)
V. Conclusion (5:12-14)

Section 5
Letters Combating
False Teachings

*. . . remain at Ephesus that you may
charge certain persons not to teach
any different doctrine, nor to
occupy themselves with myths and
endless genealogies which
promote speculations rather than
the divine training that is in faith;
whereas the aim of our
charge is love that issues from a
pure heart and a good
conscience and sincere faith.*

1 Timothy 1:3-5

19
First, Second, and Third John

Author: Same as the Gospel of John (?)
Date: About A.D. 100
Place: From Ephesus (?)
Theme: The distinguishing marks of true Christianity are love for one another and genuine faith in the material reality of Jesus Christ.

"Beloved, let us love one another; for love is of God, and he who loves is born of God and knows God. He who does not love does not know God; for God is love" (1 John 4:7-8). That's just one of several passages in First John that leaps out and grabs the reader with its powerful simplicity. This relatively brief letter (five chapters) is a beautiful statement of the basic fundamentals of the Christian faith and way, and the writer has expressed his message so well that there is little chance that the reader will misunderstand.

Second John is a brief note (13 verses) of rejoicing and encouragement for a particular group within a particular church who had remained faithful through a confrontation with a serious challenge to the fundamentals of the Christian faith and way. Second John also reveals the nature of that challenge: "For many deceivers have gone out into the world, men who will not acknowledge the coming of Jesus Christ in the flesh . . ." (v. 7). This is a clear reference to the heretical perversion of Christianity known as Gnosticism.

Gnosticism gets its name from the Greek word for a special kind of knowledge or wisdom. According to the Gnostics, salvation depends upon this "gnosis," or special knowledge, that comes as a gift from God. They believed that the material, physical world is evil. Therefore, it was unthinkable to them that Christ could have really had a physical body that actually suffered and died. They claimed that Christ only *seemed* to have a physical body and that he only *seemed* to suffer and die. This is what John was talking about when he referred to "men who will not acknowledge the coming of Jesus Christ *in the flesh.*" He was not talking about those who deny that Jesus ever lived; he was talking about those who claimed that he only *seemed* to be fully human.

Many Gnostics also believed that since salvation depended upon possession of the special kind of knowledge or wisdom, physical conduct in the body was of no consequence. The only thing that mattered was possessing that secret knowledge. A person who had that knowledge didn't have to be concerned about such things as morality or sin. It was this feature of Gnosticism that the writer of these letters was talking about when he said things such as, "If we say we have no sin, we deceive ourselves, and the truth is not in us" (1 John 1:8).

Gnosticism was gaining influence and followers during the time when the New Testament was being written, and it continued to be a problem for a century or more afterward. It was part of the problem Paul had to deal with in his letter to the Colossians and is referred to indirectly in several other New Testament books, including the Gospel of John. But in these letters of John the problem of Gnosticism was attacked head-on.

Both Second and Third John reflect a serious split of local churches—possibly the same church—into two factions, each of which refused to entertain or listen to visiting speakers or missionaries representing the viewpoint of the opposing faction.

The writer of these letters expressed his gratitude to the faction of the church, in Second John, and to an individual, in Third John, who had welcomed visiting missionaries representing his viewpoint. First John is the positive statement of his viewpoint, and, as already noted, it is a beautiful and powerful statement of the basic fundamentals of the Christian faith and way. The opposite faction referred to in all these letters was Gnosticism.

Don't make too much of that split. It's possible to miss the extremely important positive message contained in these letters if we try to understand them exclusively in terms of a reaction against Gnosticism. The growing influence of that heresy merely provided the need and opportunity for this very gifted writer to proclaim in no uncertain terms the real truth about the character of God and our proper relationship to Him.

There is a wide range of opinions concerning the identity of this very gifted writer. Many scholars believe that he was the apostle John. Others believe that he was a friend and associate of the apostle. The problem of identifying the writer is further complicated by the fact that the author of Revelation and the author of one of the Gospels were also named John. Some scholars believe that all these books were written by the same John. Others believe that they were all written by different Johns. Certain similarities of language and ideas indicate the probability that the Gospel and these letters were written by the same person, but Revelation was probably written by someone else—another John. Fortunately, it is not necessary to know with certainty the identity of the author in order to understand any of these books.

It may be worth mentioning that the writer seems to claim that he personally witnessed the life of Jesus: "the life was made manifest, and we saw it . . ." (1 John 1:2; see also vv. 3, 5). He may have, indeed, been reminding his readers that he had personally seen and heard Jesus. More probably, he was reminding them that "we," meaning our side of this controversy, can trace our beliefs back directly to Jesus, whereas "they," the Gnostics, have picked up a lot of their beliefs from pagan religions and philosophies.

Outline

(one sitting suggested to read all three books)

First John: I. Introduction (1:1-4)
              II. Light and Darkness (1:5-2:17)
              III. Truth and Falsehood (2:18-29)
              IV. Children of God and Children of the
                   Devil (3:1-10)
              V. Love Is the True Test of Christianity
                   (3:11-5:12)
              VI. Conclusion (5:13-21)

Second John: I. Greetings (vv. 1-3)
              II. Importance of Love (vv. 4-6)
              III. Warning Against Error (vv. 7-11)
              IV. Conclusion (vv. 12-13)

Third John: I. Greetings (v. 1)
              II. Praise of Gaius (vv. 2-8)
              III. Condemnation of Diotrephes (vv. 9-11)
              IV. Conclusion (vv. 12-15)

20
First and Second Timothy and Titus

Author: Admirer of Paul (?)
Date: A.D. 100–150
Place: Rome (?)
Theme: The importance of qualified leaders and sound teachings in the church

These three letters are referred to as the pastoral letters because they are the only books in the New Testament written specifically for Christian ministers, or pastors. They seem to share the general purpose of preparing Timothy and Titus for their roles as ministers in the early church. However, things are not always what they seem. Careful reading soon reveals that the main purpose of these letters was to combat false teachings and practices which were spreading through the church.' The importance of teaching "sound doctrine" was emphasized as something more than merely a guiding principle for ministers; it was a positive exhortation to root out the false and divisive elements which were threatening the life and significance of the church.

Because of their many similarities, these three letters are

usually grouped together and considered as a unit. That may be a mistake. The weight of evidence for Second Timothy, when taken by itself, seems to suggest that it may well be what it appears to be, namely, a personal letter written by Paul near the end of his life to his younger associate minister, Timothy.

But the stronger and more prevalent evidence for First Timothy and Titus indicates that at least these two letters were written by someone living several decades after Paul had died. They were written during a time when the church was being torn apart by false teachings and false teachers. The writer was a great admirer of Paul who remembered how strongly Paul had opposed the false teachers and teachings of his own day. He composed these letters in order to bring the prestige and authority of Paul into the struggle against currently popular false teachers and teachings.

It should be remembered that it was a completely legitimate and accepted practice of that time for later admirers to write under the name of some famous personality. That was the method by which the teachings of the famous personality were applied to contemporary problems and concerns. These pastoral letters, at least First Timothy and Titus, are almost surely examples of that practice.

Ordinarily, the identity of the author of any given New Testament book is relatively unimportant. The really important thing is what it says, not who said it. However, if we try to fit our understanding of these pastoral letters into the assumption that they were written by Paul, we will not only misunderstand what they are saying, but we will also introduce a false element into our understanding of what Paul said elsewhere.

These letters propose to combat false teachers and teachings by strengthening church organization and administration. Loyalty to the established church was presented as the test for the genuineness of personal religion, and commitment to the peaceful progress and prosperity of the institutional church and its accepted teachings had become the highest priority of the Christian life. Somehow, that just doesn't sound like the apostle Paul.

In these letters, "faith" often refers to the acceptance of a set body of doctrinal beliefs. It is incredible that Paul, who had elsewhere so emphatically proclaimed faith as a matter of radical, trusting confidence and spiritual union with Jesus Christ, could now discuss faith in terms of "sound doctrine." It is very difficult to believe that the man who wrote these letters is the same man who wrote, for example, Romans 6–8.

Also, notice how often the Holy Spirit is *not* mentioned in these letters. In a discussion of the life of the Christian church, with particular attention to the qualifications, selection, and responsibilities of church leaders, Paul would ordinarily be expected to give strong emphasis to the Holy Spirit as the supreme guide and source of strength and wisdom. It's almost a shock to find the Holy Spirit ignored in such statements as "This charge I commit to you, Timothy, my son, in accordance with the prophetic utterances which pointed to you, that inspired by them you may wage the good warfare" (1 Timothy 1:18). Surely Paul would have given the Holy Spirit at least equal credit with "prophetic utterances" for inspiring Timothy for his work, not to mention pointing to him in the first place!

Again, in the same letter we read, "Do not neglect the gift you have, which was given you by prophetic utterance when the council of elders laid their hands upon you" (4:14). Notice that Timothy is reported to have received his gift not from the Holy Spirit but from "prophetic utterance," and he received that gift not when he was filled with the Holy Spirit but "when the council of elders laid their hands upon [him]." Paul would never have said it like that; he would never have given more credit to the words and acts of the church establishment than to the Holy Spirit!

But someone with less spiritual insight than the apostle Paul, living many years later when the church was old enough to have an establishment, would almost be expected to say it like that. By that time, even the false teachers were claiming the Holy Spirit as their guide. Therefore, the writer appealed to a more distinctive authentication of Timothy's ministry: ordination by the established, orthodox church—"when the elders laid their hands upon you."

There are several such places throughout these letters where we might expect Paul to mention the Holy Spirit; but the Spirit is mentioned as an active, guiding force only three times, once in each letter: 1 Timothy 4:1; 2 Timothy 1:14; and Titus 3:5-6.

It's also interesting to compare 1 Timothy 2:14—"And Adam was not deceived, but the woman was deceived and became a transgressor"—with Romans 5:14-19. In First Timothy, Adam is absolved and all the blame is placed on the woman; in Romans, Paul places the blame on the man Adam, and Eve is not even mentioned. It's not an irreconcilable conflict, but it's a very strange difference if we try to assume that the same man wrote both passages.

In this introduction to these pastoral letters we have concentrated our attention too exclusively perhaps on their contrasts with the teachings of Paul. When we come actually to read them, it will be a tragic loss to us if we find nothing but these contrasts. The main message of these letters is that the church must *believe* in something if it is to maintain its power and significance in the world and that *what* it believes must be thoroughly and firmly grounded in the teachings, the "sound doctrine," of those who have historically and personally experienced that power and significance in Jesus Christ. These letters also remind us that in order to maintain that belief, the church must be very careful in the selection of genuinely qualified and responsible leaders.

The apostle Paul would have agreed—and, in other contexts, did agree—with that message. The fact that there are reasons to believe that someone with less spiritual insight than Paul actually wrote these letters is no reason to reject their message. After all, one can have much valuable insight and still have less than Paul.

The main value of these letters is to show us how early Christians responded to the divisive influence of false teachings in the church. Perhaps the most important lesson we can learn from them is that there is such a thing as false teaching and that when false teaching invades the church, the Christian faith loses some of its power and significance. Regardless of who wrote them, there is an extremely important truth in the warning words of 2 Timothy 4:3-4.

Outline

(one sitting suggested to read all three books)

First Timothy: I. Greetings (1:1-2)

21
Jude and
Second Peter

Authors:?
Dates: About A.D. 125 and 150
Places: Rome (?)
Theme: Condemnation of false teachings and immoral practices in the church and an appeal for a firm stand in the faith and practices taught by the original apostles

These two brief letters were written to combat the same Gnostic heresy that John had been concerned about in his letters. By the time Jude and Second Peter were written, the problem was even worse. For John, the phase of Gnosticism that seemed to be the greatest concern was the heretical belief that Christians were distinguished by possession of a special kind of knowledge or wisdom, the "gnosis." The greatest concern for the writers of Jude and Second Peter was the immorality fostered by the Gnostic belief that possession of the gnosis lifted Christians above such mundane things as morals and ethics.

Jude was written about A.D. 125. It was not really a letter but was more of a general tract addressed to all Christians. Jude had intended to write about the more fundamental subject of Christian salvation, but he became so disturbed by false members and teachers within the church that he changed his mind and wrote about that problem instead. He appeals to true believers "to contend for the faith which was once for all delivered to the saints" (v. 3) and then launches into an attack on those "ungodly persons who pervert the grace of our God into licentiousness and deny our only Master and Lord, Jesus Christ" (v. 4). He later says that these ungodly persons are "blemishes on your love feasts, as they boldly carouse together, looking after themselves; waterless clouds, carried along by winds; fruitless trees in late autumn, twice dead, uprooted; wild waves of the sea, casting up the foam of their own shame; wandering stars for whom the nether gloom of darkness has been reserved for ever" (vv. 12-13). He didn't like them!

Second Peter was written about A.D. 150 and was the last of the New Testament books to be written. Even though it claims to be from the hand of the apostle Peter, in several places it betrays a date much later than Peter. Perhaps the strongest evidence for a later date is the reference to things Paul had said "in all his letters" (3:16). That reference makes it clear that a collection of Paul's letters had already been made and distributed before Second Peter was written. Later in the same verse, the writer says that some people twist the teachings of Paul's letters "as they do the other scriptures." When this was written, Paul's letters had not only been collected together, but they were also considered part of the Christian "scripture." None of that happened until long after Peter had died. Second Peter is another example of a later admirer writing under the name of a famous personality. Since this writer was trying to call the church back to the teachings of the original apostles, he chose to write under the name of the most famous apostle of all.

Second Peter, like Jude, attacks the false teachings and immoral practices of the Gnostics. The author also reminds his readers that "the day of the Lord will come like a thief, and then the heavens will pass away with a loud noise, and the elements will be dissolved with fire, and the earth and the works that are upon it will be burned up" (3:10). Belief that Christ would return soon was very strong during the earliest days of Christianity, but as time passed and it didn't happen, many people began to doubt that he would return at all. Second Peter interprets it as a sign that the end is near when scoffers begin saying, "Where is the promise of his coming? For ever since the fathers fell asleep, all things have continued as they were from the beginning of creation" (3:4). The writer answers the scoffers by telling them, in effect, not to become too cocky; he'll be here soon—so they'd best start getting ready!

The chief value of these two letters is their strong emphasis upon the importance of religious beliefs. What we believe determines how we live. The false beliefs of the Gnostics led them into lives of immorality and meaninglessness—they became "mists driven by a storm" (2:17). The true beliefs of genuine Christians led them to be "without spot or blemish, and at peace" (3:14).

Outline
(one sitting suggested to read both books)

Jude:
    I. Introduction (vv. 1-4)
    II. Condemnation of Heretics (vv. 5-16)
    III. Stand Firm in the True Faith (vv. 17-23)
    IV. Benediction (vv. 24-25)

Second Peter:
    I. Introduction (1:1-2)
    II. Stand Firm in the True Faith (1:3-21)
    III. Condemnation of Heretics (2:1-22)
    IV. Second Coming of Christ (3:1-18)

Section 6
Special Books

Take care, brethren, lest there be in any of you an evil, unbelieving heart, leading you to fall away from the living God. But exhort one another every day, as long as it is called "today," that none of you may be hardened by the deceitfulness of sin.

Hebrews 3:12-13

22
Hebrews

Author: ?
Date: A.D. 70–100
Place: Either to or from Rome(?)
Theme: Christianity is the perfect religion.

Many people, including some reputable scholars, make the mistake of trying to read the entire Christian message into the book of Hebrews. In fact, Hebrews is often described as the proclamation of the Christian message to Jews in much the same way that Paul's letter to the Romans was the proclamation of the Christian message to Gentiles. That view overshoots the mark in its effort to find the key to understanding Hebrews.

Paul's letter to the Romans is a comprehensive presentation of the basic, essential elements of his version of the Christian faith and way. The writer of Hebrews states very explicitly that he is not talking about the basic essentials when he says, "Therefore let us leave the elementary doctrine of Christ and go on to maturity, not laying again a foundation of repentance from dead works and of faith toward God" (6:1). Later in that same passage, the writer of

Hebrews gives us the key to understanding what he was trying to do: "For it is impossible to restore again to repentance those who have once been enlightened, who have tasted the heavenly gift, . . . if they then commit apostasy . . ." (6:4-6).

The purpose of Hebrews was to encourage readers to stand firm in the faith: "Take care, brethren, lest there be in any of you an evil, unbelieving heart, leading you to fall away from the living God" (3:12). Time and again throughout the book, the writer reveals his deep concern that his readers may lose out on the glorious benefits of the Christian faith by drifting into complacency or false beliefs—or perhaps even back into Judaism. To halt that tendency and prevent what he considered its tragic and irreversible consequences, the writer develops the theme that Christianity is the perfect religion, fulfilling the promise (promises) of Judaism and thus making it obsolete. We could say that his main point was that anything Judaism did, Christianity does better. He also lifts up the perfection of Christianity as the thing that makes it worth enduring the sacrifices and persecutions which other Christians had faced in the past and which his readers were apparently about to face in the present or immediate future (12:1-29).

To support his view that Christianity is the perfect religion, the writer of Hebrews points to its roots which reach deeply into the past, all the way back to Abraham. He calls the roll of heroes from the past and points out that they all found power and meaning for life in their times through faith in God's promises, which have now been fulfilled in Jesus. He goes into great detail to show that Jesus is the perfect and complete High Priest who made the perfect and complete sacrifice for all sins for all time. He says all this not to persuade his readers to become Christians—he assumes throughout that they have already done that—but, rather, to persuade them to *stay* Christians. He argues that Christianity is the only true religion that offers the only true way to live with the only true God. All other religions—along with their priests, ritual sacrifices, and other rites and practices—are not only inferior but are actually false. "Therefore, since we are surrounded by so great a cloud of witnesses, let us also lay aside every weight, and sin which clings so closely, and let us run with perseverance the race that is set before us, looking to Jesus the pioneer and perfecter of our faith, who for the joy that was set before him endured the cross, despising the shame, and is seated at the right hand of the throne of God" (12:1-2).

Undoubtedly the most famous and oft-quoted verse in Hebrews is 11:1: "Now faith is the assurance of things hoped for, the conviction of things not seen." The meaning of that verse is made somewhat clearer in *The New English Bible:* "And what is faith? Faith gives substance to our hopes, and makes us certain of realities we do not see." It's made clearer still by *The Living Bible:* "What is faith? It is the confident assurance that something we want is going to happen. It is the certainty that what we hope for is waiting for us, even though we cannot see it up ahead." Needless to say, this one verse, as profoundly true as it is, is not the complete definition of Christian faith. It was never intended to be.

There has always been much uncertainty about the identity of the author of Hebrews. The earliest manuscripts do not identify the author. It was eventually credited to Paul at the insistence of those who believed that he wrote it. Even then, however, there were many who did not believe that he wrote it. That uncertainty about the identity of the author has continued through the centuries and will doubtless continue on through the future. Martin Luther, for example, believed that it was written by Apollos. Several other possibilities have been suggested, but there is probably no way that we can ever know for sure. While it is extremely doubtful that Paul wrote it, we should be very grateful that he was given credit for it. Otherwise, it probably would not have been included in the New Testament.

There is also much uncertainty about the date it was written. A variety of scholarly theories support a wide range of dates. The most likely date seems to be about A.D. 90. If that date is correct, the past persecutions of Christians referred to by the writer would be the Roman persecution under the emperor Nero; the persecutions which the readers were about to face would be those under the emperor Domitian.

Other uncertainties about Hebrews include its point of origin and its destination. A reference at the close of the book seems to relate one or the other to the church at Rome: "Those who come from Italy send you greetings" (13:24). This could mean that it was written in Rome and that the Italians were sending greetings to their fellow Christians in another country; or it could mean that native Italians living in another country were sending greetings to folks back home. Take your choice.

Outline:

(two sittings suggested to read the entire book)

Sitting One:
    I. Superiority of Jesus
      A. Compared to Prophets (1:1-3)
      B. Compared to Angels (1:4-2:18)
      C. Compared to Moses (3:1-4:13)
    II. The True High Priest
      A. The Priesthood Itself (4:14-7:28)

Sitting Two:
      B. The Covenant (8:1-9:10)
      C. The Sacrifice (9:11-10:39)
    III. Importance of Faith
      A. Examples from the Past (Chapter 11)
      B. Significance for the Present (Chapter 12)
    IV. Personal Exhortation and Benediction (Chapter 13)

23
The Revelation
to John

Author: A courageous Christian named John
Date: A.D. 95–96
Place: Patmos (or Ephesus after his return from Patmos)
Theme: Christians who stand firm for Christ through the wicked Roman oppression and persecutions will receive indescribably glorious blessings and rewards.

To understand the book of Revelation at all, we must understand it as a whole. While it can be divided rather neatly into separate and more or less distinct scenes, the real meaning and message begins to come through only when all the scenes have run their course. One of the big reasons so many of us find Revelation so difficult and mysterious is that we try to understand it before we learn it.

When reading Revelation, it's very helpful to "see" John's vision exactly as he describes it. Read it as though it were the script for a dramatic stage or screen presentation. Visualize in your own imagination the Spirit of Christ dictating letters, the Lamb breaking seals on a scroll, angels blowing trumpets, the beast with seven heads and ten horns, and all the rest. Try to imagine that you are watching everything being played out on a giant movie screen with stereophonic sound.

In the first scene (1:1–3:22), Christ dictates letters to seven churches in Asia Minor. These letters set the stage for what is to follow by reminding each of the churches of its strengths and weaknesses and promising rich rewards to everyone who stands firm until the final victory.

The second scene (4:1–8:1) reveals that many of the troubles on earth are the result of a great cosmic war between the spiritual forces of good and the spiritual forces of evil that are raging throughout the universe. This scene, wherein the Lamb breaks the seven seals on the scroll, also shows God's servants on earth being marked with a seal upon their foreheads. This seal assures them that they have nothing to fear from subsequent suffering or horrors which are still to come.

The third scene (8:2–11:19) shows the cosmic war increasing in intensity and the earth becoming a major battlefield. This scene, in which seven angels blow seven trumpets, ends with God laying claim to earth as his territory: ". . . the kingdom of the world has become the kingdom of our Lord and of his Christ, and he shall reign for ever and ever" (11:15). God is not going to surrender earth to the forces of evil. It is his, and he is going to keep it!

The fourth scene (12:1–14:20) opens with the dragon (Satan) being thwarted in his scheme to devour a woman's newborn child on earth. The dragon is then defeated in heaven and thrown down to earth. The great cosmic war is now concentrated upon earth, with the dragon, the beast, and their followers on one side and the Lamb and his followers on the other.

In scene five (15:1–16:21), angels pour out seven bowls of God's wrath upon the earth. This wrath is aimed at those who bear the mark of the beast. The forces of evil, represented by the dragon and the beast, are making their last stand. Near the end of this scene, an alliance of the dragon, the beast, and false prophets gathers kings from all over the world in preparation for the final battle. This is their last chance, and they gather at a place called Armageddon (16:16). When the seventh bowl of wrath is poured out, a voice calls from the throne of the temple, "It is done!" There is lightning, thunder, an earthquake, and huge hailstones. The nations fall.

Scene six (17:1-20:15) shows the eternal horrifying doom that finally comes to "the great harlot who is seated upon many waters, with whom the kings of the earth have committed fornication" (17:1-2) and upon "Babylon the great, mother of harlots and of earth's abominations" (17:5). Also shown in this scene is the defeat and imprisonment of Satan and his ultimate, final destruction. This leaves God completely triumphant and supreme in all the earth as well as in all the universe.

But there's even greater glory in store for those who are written in the Lamb's book of life, those who have stood firmly with him through everything. The final scene (21:1-22:21) shows the arrival of a new age in which this earth and even heaven are replaced by a "holy city, new Jerusalem, coming down out of heaven from God, prepared as a bride adorned for her husband" (21:2). There is no death, no crying, no pain in this holy city, "for the former things have passed away" (21:4). "Nothing unclean shall enter it, nor any one who practices abomination or falsehood, but only those who are written in the Lamb's book of life" (21:27). "And night shall be no more; they need no light of lamp or sun, for the Lord God will be their light, and they shall reign for ever and ever" (22:5). End of vision!

We can avoid much, if not most, of the thick confusion that surrounds the book of Revelation today if we will accept it as what it claims to be: the written description of a vision that the writer, John, saw and heard concerning the spiritual significance and ultimate outcome of the terrible things taking place during his lifetime.

John introduces his description of the vision he saw while on the island of Patmos by explaining that it is "the revelation of Jesus Christ, which God gave him to show to his servants what must soon take place . . ." (1:1). He goes on to pronounce a blessing on those who read aloud, who hear, and who keep "what is written therein; for the time is near" (1:3). In the last chapter, after the description of the vision proper, John records that he heard Jesus say no less than three times, "I am coming soon" (22:7, 12, and 20). In addition to that, John was specifically instructed to leave his book unsealed because "the time is near" (22:10).

It could not have been made more clear or more definite that John's vision concerned the things that were happening then and there! The book of Revelation is not the history of the world written in advance; it is the powerful proclamation in very dramatic form of the eternal truth that God is supreme and his goodness will ultimately triumph regardless of how strong and deeply entrenched evil may seem to be.

It took a lot of faith for Christians in John's day to believe that. They saw evil firmly entrenched upon the throne of the world in the form of the Roman Empire that was conquering, persecuting, and apparently destroying everything good and decent. The Roman emperor Domitian had even set himself up as divine, insisting that he be worshiped as "our Lord and God." Christians who refused to worship the emperor were being severely persecuted. That's why John was on the island of Patmos. He was sent there because he insisted upon worshiping God and Christ rather than the emperor. There was very little visible indication that the Christian faith and way would even be able to survive, let alone have any significant influence in the world. All the power and armies and authority of Rome were aligned solidly on the side of evil, and Rome ruled the world. How could a scattered minority of Christians hope to hang on against such tremendous odds? John's vision as recorded in the book of Revelation answers that question.

In his vision, John saw, and afterwards wrote to tell other Christians, that wicked Rome (the "beast rising out of the sea, with ten horns and seven heads," "the great harlot who is seated upon many waters," "Babylon the great, mother of harlots and of earth's abominations") which was allied with Satan ("the dragon") was doomed. Rome was doomed because the earth belongs to God and Christ and they will not forever endure the Roman sacrilege and wickedness. God's triumph is sure, and those who stand firm with God and Christ through this Roman persecution will share in God's triumph; those who do not stand firm with God and Christ will share Rome's doom.

The book of Revelation is a powerful reminder for every age that worldly pleasure and pain, success and failure, comfort and suffering, are all always very tentative and temporary; the only thing really important in life is to be aligned with the truth and goodness and power of God and of his Christ. If we do that, nothing, not even death, can harm us; if we fail to be so aligned, nothing can save us.

John's vision shows very little of God's compassion. On the contrary, it shows a warlord using some of the most horrifying methods imaginable to defeat a hated enemy. That's not at all like the God we see revealed in the life, suffering, death, and resurrection of Jesus Christ. But John's vision is not concerned with the personality or character traits of God as much as with his eternal supremacy. The real meaning and message of Revelation is that regardless of how strong and deeply entrenched evil may be in this world, God and his goodness will ultimately triumph here as well as in heaven.

Outline

(two sittings suggested to read the entire book)

Sitting One: I. Letters to Seven Churches (Chapters 1-3)
            II. Breaking the Seven Seals (4:1–8:1)
            III. Seven Trumpet Blasts (8:2–11:19)

Sitting Two: IV. The Dragon Is Thrown to Earth (Chapters 12-14)
            V. Bowls of Wrath (Chapters 15-16)
            VI. The Harlot's Doom and God's Triumph (Chapters 17-20)
            VII. The New Age (Chapters 21-22)